D0758176

Migration, Minorities and Citizenship
General Editors: **Zig Layton-Henry**, Professor of Politics, University of Warwick; and **Danièle Joly**, Professor, Director, Centre for Research in Ethnic Relations, University of Warwick

Titles include:

Rutvica Andrijasevic
MIGRATION, AGENCY AND CITZENSHIP IN SEX TRAFFICKING

Muhammad Anwar, Patrick Roach and Ranjit Sondhi (*editors*)
FROM LEGISLATION TO INTEGRATION?
Race Relations in Britain

James A. Beckford, Danièle Joly and Farhad Khosrokhavar
MUSLIMS IN PRISON
Challenge and Change in Britain and France

Gideon Calder, Phillip Cole, Jonathan Seglow
CITIZENSHIP ACQUISITION NATIONAL BELONGING
Migration, Membership and the Liberal Democratic State

Thomas Faist and Andreas Ette (*editors*)
THE EUROPEANIZATION OF NATIONAL POLICIES AND POLITICS
OF IMMIGRATION
Between Autonomy and the European Union

Thomas Faist and Peter Kivisto (*editors*)
DUAL CITIZENSHIP IN GLOBAL PERSPECTIVE
From Unitary to Multiple Citizenship

Adrian Favell
PHILOSOPHIES OF INTEGRATION
Immigration and the Idea of Citizenship in France and Britain

Agata Górny and Paulo Ruspini (*editors*)
MIGRATION IN THE NEW EUROPE
East-West Revisited

James Hampshire
CITIZENSHIP AND BELONGING
Immigration and the Politics of Democratic Governance in Postwar Britain

John R. Hinnells (*editor*)
RELIGIOUS RECONSTRUCTION IN THE SOUTH ASIAN DIASPORAS
From One Generation to Another

Ayhan Kaya
ISLAM, MIGRATION AND INTEGRATION
The Age of Securitization

Zig Layton-Henry and Czarina Wilpert (*editors*)
CHALLENGING RACISM IN BRITAIN AND GERMANY

Jørgen S. Nielsen
TOWARDS A EUROPEAN ISLAM

Pontus Odmalm
MIGRATION POLICIES AND POLITICAL PARTICIPATION
Inclusion or Intrusion in western Europe?

Prodromos Panayiotopoulos
ETHNICITY, MIGRATION AND ENTERPRISE

Aspasia Papadopoulou-Kourkoula
TRANSIT MIGRATION
The Missing Link Between Emigration and Settlement

Jan Rath (*editor*)
IMMIGRANT BUSINESSES
The Economic, Political and Social Environment

Carl-Ulrik Schierup (*editor*)
SCRAMBLE FOR THE BALKANS
Nationalism, Globalism and the Political Economy of Reconstruction

Vicki Squire
THE EXCLUSIONARY POLITICS OF ASYLUM

Maarten Vink
LIMITS OF EUROPEAN CITIZENSHIP
European Integration and Domestic Immigration Policies

Östen Wahlbeck
KURDISH DIASPORAS
A Comparative Study of Kurdish Refugee Communities

Lucy Williams
GLOBAL MARRIAGE
Cross-Border Marriage Migration in Global Context

Migration, Minorities and Citizenship
Series Standing Order ISBN 978–0–333–71047–0 (hardback) and
978–0–333–80338–7 (paperback)
(*outside North America only*)

You can receive future titles in this series as they are published by placing a standing order. Please contact your bookseller or, in case of difficulty, write to us at the address below with your name and address, the title of the series and the ISBN quoted above.

Customer Services Department, Macmillan Distribution Ltd, Houndmills, Basingstoke, Hampshire RG21 6XS, England

---

Migration, Agency and Citizenship in Sex Trafficking

Rutvica Andrijasevic
Open University, UK

First published 2010 by
PALGRAVE MACMILLAN

Palgrave Macmillan in the UK is an imprint of Macmillan Publishers Limited, registered in England, company number 785998, of Houndmills, Basingstoke, Hampshire RG21 6XS.

Palgrave Macmillan in the US is a division of St Martin's Press LLC, 175 Fifth Avenue, New York, NY 10010.

Palgrave Macmillan is the global academic imprint of the above companies and has companies and representatives throughout the world.

Palgrave® and Macmillan® are registered trademarks in the United States, the United Kingdom, Europe and other countries.

ISBN 978–0–230–23740–7   hardback

This book is printed on paper suitable for recycling and made from fully managed and sustained forest sources. Logging, pulping and manufacturing processes are expected to conform to the environmental regulations of the country of origin.

A catalogue record for this book is available from the British Library.

Library of Congress Cataloging-in-Publication Data

Andrijasevic, Rutvica, 1972–

Migration, agency and citizenship in sex trafficking / Rutvica Andrijasevic.
        p. cm. — (Migration, minorities and citizenship)
        ISBN 978–0–230–23740–7
        1. Human trafficking—Europe.   2. Women foreign workers—Europe.   3. Prostitution—Europe.   4. Women—Europe—Social conditions.   I. Title.
        HQ281.A53 2010
        306.74'2094—dc22

                                                                                2010027482

10   9   8   7   6   5   4   3   2   1
19   18   17   16   15   14   13   12   11   10

Printed and bound in Great Britain by
CPI Antony Rowe, Chippenham and Eastbourne

To my parents, Ani and Jadran

Contents

(Instead of a) Preface

The decision

Liudmila hated the job because it was not as she had imagined it. She worked on the streets, did exhausting shifts and was not free to come and go as she pleased. Yes, she was in Italy but it did not feel like it. She spent most of her nights on the streets and most of her days at the Residence. She was in Bologna but saw nothing of the city and met no one but clients. She hated it. She worried that no man would ever want to marry her and have children with her because they would think of her as a whore.

Luigi, a regular client she befriended, urged her to leave sex work and live with him. At first, Liudmila was not sure whether to trust him, but as he kept coming and looking for her, she decided to accept his offer. She got hold of her passport from where the third party was keeping it and rang Luigi to pick her up. It was in the middle of the day and Luigi was working. He said that the moment was rather inconvenient and that he would come later. This did not go down well with Liudmila. She told him that if he was not picking her up, she would walk. She would walk. Shortly afterwards Luigi did indeed pick Liudmila up. They drove to his brother's place, where he offered to host them.

Leaving Moldova

When at college, Liudmila had already had a bad marriage behind her and little money or prospects. She met her ex-husband at the age of 16, married at 18 and divorced at 19. A year after her divorce, she left Moldova for Italy hoping to find a new partner. A girlfriend of hers, who had left for Italy not long before, kept on telling Liudmila that Italy was a good place to live. The friend worked as a sex worker, met a man she fell in love with and was very happy. After she lost her job as a secretary at Sidis, an Italian owned supermarket chain in Moldova, Liudmila decided to leave for Italy. Her boss, an Italian man notorious for hitting on all women that worked for him, laid Liudmila off after she turned him down. Having no job made things really difficult for her. She was now without any income. The money she was paid was not much, 20 Euro a month and barely sufficient to live on. The work was stressful and tough. She started her shift at 9 am and finished at 8 pm. 'Such long hours and they still treat you like shit', she commented, remembering the job at the supermarket. But it permitted her to pay her monthly costs and get by. She did not need to pay rent. The flat she lived in was her father's.

Having met Italians at work and reassured by her friend that Italy was a good place to be, Liudmila decided to give it a go. By this time she had left university. She could not make ends meet and did not want to ask her father for money. The friend living in Italy sent her money so that she could arrange for the visa and travel. She also promised to help Liudmila look for a job once she got to Bologna. Liudmila contacted agencies arranging tourist visas, but none was able to get her one because of the NATO bombings of Serbia. After several months of trying to get a visa Liudmila still did not have one, had no job, and had spent all the money the friend had given her. There was a way around this, a friend told her, and she put Liudmila in touch with an agent who would organise her travel to Italy. In return she would have to do sex work. Liudmila met the agent and agreed on a three-month contract for sex work. She would be working for someone in Bologna she did not know. Liudmila agreed to earn 120000 EUR in three months; 1200 EUR was hers to keep. She could have her travel back home paid for after three months or, alternatively, could stay and work for three more months and keep all the money for herself. Soon afterwards Liudmila left for Italy. She arrived first in Budapest where she met seven other women. The groups travelled further by a van. They took sleeping pills and laid low at the bottom of the van so that the border police would not see them. Once in Slovenia, they walked though the forest and over the border to reach Italy, where another van was waiting for them. After four days of travel, Liudmila arrived at the Residence in Bologna where she would stay one month and work in street prostitution.

Establishing relationships

Luigi was not the only client with whom Liudmila became intimately involved. The third party she worked for did not allow women to socialise with clients outside their working hours. But Liudmila was able to bend the rules when it came to Roberto, with whom she spent quite some time after her shifts. She made it look as if he was just like any other client. She would collect her money from Roberto and they would go to his place to have sex, chat, watch TV, cook and so on.

Liudmila enjoyed these breaks from a routine of tiring shifts and third party control. She worked on the streets each night from 7 pm until 5 am. On Sundays the shift was slightly shorter – until 2 am. At the end of the shift she would be exhausted. She would go to the Residence where she and the other women lived and sleep until her next shift. Then she would get ready to work again. All of the women always went to work and back again together. The new ones, including Liudmila, were instructed by those who had been there for a longer period of time about what the job was about. What to do, how to ask for money and how to keep safe.

Liudmila missed Roberto when she quit sex work and was staying with Luigi. Her living arrangements kept changing. At first she stayed with Luigi's brother. He was dating a woman from Moldova who had previously worked in street prostitution too. They all stayed together for several weeks in the brother's flat until some friends of his went on holiday. They gave Liudmila the keys to their place and let her stay there for another couple of weeks. When they returned, she found accommodation in a catholic institute run by the Don Benzi organisation, a priest famous in Italy for his mission to save women trafficked into the sex industry.

In the meantime, Liudmila had decided that she wanted to stay in Italy. She went to talk to the police and several NGOs to get information on how she could do that. The police sent her away. The NGOs suggested that she press charges against the third party and request a residence permit for victims of trafficking. This permit would allow her to stay and work in Italy for at least six months or possibly longer. Liudmila then went to the women's shelter and inquired about what pressing charges exactly entailed and what would be the gains. After a couple of weeks she decided in favour of it and asked for housing at the women's shelter. Luigi could no longer host her and she did not want to return to the Catholic institute from which she just run away. 'Living there was like being in prison', she said. Every day she had to get up at 7 am and spent most of the day cleaning the premises. She and the others were not allowed to leave the institute and could not have any contact with the outside world, not even receive phone calls. Luigi managed to speak to Liudmila only after prolonged insistence. When he finally did get through to her, they agreed that she needed to leave the institute and that he would come and get her.

Meanwhile, Roberto was away on holiday in the south of Italy, visiting his family. He and Liudmila phoned regularly. When one day she told him that she was missing him really badly, Roberto interrupted his holidays and returned to Bologna. Liudmila ended her relationship with Luigi and started one with Roberto. She considered him to be in love with her. She was very happy with their sex life. Roberto admired greatly her ability to give him pleasure. That was very important to Liudmila. She compared it to the sex she used to have with her ex husband, which she referred to as boring and bland. She commented on the sex she had with her ex-husband: 'It was one of those things, you look at the ceiling and let him do'. After the time she spent doing sex work, she saw herself as an expert in the field. She could now tell what men liked and was more aware of what type of person each of them was. Liudmila had become very good at meeting men's expectations.

The relationship with Roberto was going so well that his friends often asked if she had girlfriends she could introduce them to. But Liudmila would not do that. She kept the world of the women's shelter separate from that of Roberto's friends. She did not want them to know that she used to do sex work. Roberto obviously knew it, but Liudmila had not told him that she had come to Italy to do sex work. She had told him instead that she found out what type of work it was only once she had already arrived in Bologna.

Italy: Future plans

Liudmila had just met a pub owner who was looking for new bar staff. Their meeting had gone well and Liudmila was optimistic about getting a job. She was legal and even had the *tesserino sanitario* (proof of state health insurance), as the owner wanted. She liked the idea of working in a pub. She saw it as a much better opportunity than working in a factory packing Easter baskets, which is what she had been doing for the last couple of months. Alternatively, she could take up caring and cleaning for the elderly, but she was not fond of that idea and found that job too demanding and tiring.

Liudmila was looking for a better job because she wanted to work and was keen to save some money. She also wanted to visit her parents in Chisinau and introduce them to Roberto. They had been engaged for five months now and Liudmila was considering whether she should move in with Roberto. They both liked the idea of renting a flat together. He could move out from the flat he shared with another person and she could move out of the women's shelter.

Liudmila had accumulated much strength and determination in the past months, especially compared to the time when she first quit sex work. During the first weeks of being off the street, Liudmila did not go out of the flat much at all. When she did, it was only in the car with

Luigi. The idea of running into the third party she worked for was not much of a worry for her even though he lived around the corner from where she was staying. She knew that she was not of interest to the third party as she was not working for him any longer. She was also not worried that the agent who recruited her back in Moldova would threaten her family. He had been paid for organising her travel and did not care about what would happen to her from the moment his part of the job was done. What really worried Liudmila for a long time was that one of her ex-clients would see her and shame her by calling her a whore.

But even that fear was gone now that she had got a residence permit. With the residence permit she felt safe. She was not worried anymore that the police might stop her, ask her for papers and arrest and deport her. Now, with the papers, she was not fearful of being called a whore anymore because if anyone did so she would tell them that they must be mistaking her for someone else. She is not the person they think she is because she is legal and has the documents. Now, with her documents in her hands, Liudmila felt her life in Italy was about to begin properly. She could invest fully in her relationship with Roberto and finally look for a job that was not sex work or factory work. 'A proper job', as she called it.

Acknowledgements

I have been told many times that writing a book is a solitary activity, a one-person show. Far from that, this book has been a rather crowded adventure as many friends and colleagues shared with me their time, insights, knowledge and patience. First and foremost, I am thankful to the migrant women whom I interviewed and who shared their stories with me, especially as these were the stories they were trying to forget. From developing the initial ideas, to fieldwork, analysis and finally to multiple rewritings, I am grateful to all the people whose support and input made this book possible. They read and commented on previous versions of the chapters, helped me retrieve the texts I could not locate in my local library, jumped in when I needed help with translation and transcription of the interviews, hosted me during the fieldwork, took care of me at various stages of the writing process or played some Balkan beat when we all needed to relax and unwind. These are: Simon Addison, Diana Anders, Elsa Antonioni, Cagla Aykac, Elena Basile, Maria Puig de le Bellacasa, Sarah Bracke, Rosi Braidotti, Rosemarie Buikema, Marina Calloni, Esra Erdem, Seda Guerses, Elspeth Guild, Sondra Hausner, Clare Hemmings, Karin Heissler, Berenice Hernandez Hernandez, Ingrid Hoofd, Simon Hutta, Bettina Knaup, Tiziana Macinelli, PaolaGioia Macioti, Angela Melitopoulos, Sandro Mezzadra, Catherine Mills, Rebecca Nash, Brett Neilson, Julia O'Connell Davidson, Dragana Okolic, Jennifer Petzen, Nirmal Puwar, Dont Rhine, Erica Rigo, Devi Sacchetto, Tatiana Suspitsina, Ioana Szeman, Wasana Wongsurawat and Shiar Youssef.

When I needed to finalise the manuscript and take a study leave, my colleagues from the Politics Department at the Open University were of immense patience and generosity. I am thankful for the encouragement and steady support I received from Jef Huysmans, Engin Isin, Vicki Squire, Mike Saward and Claudia Aradau. Bridget Anderson, Nicola Mai, Dimitris Papadopoulos and Dag Stenvoll read my chapters on the shortest notice ever given to anyone and generously offered their time, feedback and critical comments at those final and most needed moments. Snezana Zabic generously helped with a rewriting of the (Instead of a) Preface. Thank you all for helping me sharpen the book and meet my deadline! Finally, there is one person whose presence, support, love and care made all the difference. I am deeply thankful to Claire Unwin for being my partner and for introducing me to the 'inner game'.

I am extremely grateful for the financial support and fellowship that the following institutions provided when I was writing this book: Open Society Institute, Women's Studies at Utrecht University, Department of Cultural Anthropology and European Ethnography at Frankfurt am Main University, Centre on Migration, Policy and Society at University of Oxford, Centre for European Policy Studies, Centre for Cultural Research at University of Western Sydney, Economic and Social Research Council's Postdoctoral Fellowship, European Commission Sixth Framework Programme's Marie Curie Research Grant [MEIF-CT-2006-025775] and British Academy&Association of Commonwealth Universities Grant for International Collaboration.

Many of the ideas in this book originate from my involvement with feminist and migrant activist networks, the NextGENDERation network, the Frassanito network, and no border groups and the Bologna women's shelter. I hope this book will help to keep going the conversations between these groups and networks and inspire future political interventions.

Parts of my previous work reappear in this book. Palgrave Macmillan granted permission to reproduce the material from my earlier publications. Chapter 1 contains ideas that were initially developed in 'Beautiful Dead Bodies: Gender, Migration and Representation in Anti-Trafficking Campaigns', 2007, *Feminist Review* and parts of an earlier version of Chapter 5 have previously appeared in 'Sex on the Move: Gender, Subjectivity and Differential Inclusion', 2009, *Subjectivity*.

1
Migration and Sex Work in Europe

Introduction

This book is about the ways in which current reconfiguration of the modes of governing in Europe are playing themselves out at the level of the subject and the impact they are having on individual experience of gender difference and sexuality. The topic through which I examine these transformations is that of 'sex trafficking', commonly understood as a process by means of which people are purposely recruited by use of force or deception for forced labour or exploitation in the sex sector. This book is, however, about more than 'sex trafficking'. My argument is that experiences such as that of Liudmila described in the Preface offer insight into broader transformations of state sovereignty, labour markets and citizenship arising as consequences of globalisation and European enlargement. It is the aim of this book to explore the conditions under which 'sex trafficking' comes about and is sustained, and to make visible how these conditions are connected to broader spheres of social and political life in contemporary Europe.

In order to tackle these issues, the analysis I undertake is centred on the following questions: What is the relationship between processes of re-bordering in Europe, in particular with regard to the functioning of the European Union's (EU) eastern borders and the confinement and exploitation of migrant labour in the sex sector? How has the discourse on 'sex trafficking' as a 'modern slavery' contributed to reinstalling the binary opposition between slavery and free waged labour, positing the former as characteristic of labour arrangements in non-democratic societies and the latter as typical of market relations in liberal democracies? What is the importance of gender and sexuality norms in whether migrants working

1

in the sex sector see themselves as workers and partake in collective mobilisations for sex workers' rights?

For social libertarian feminists and activists for sex workers' rights, abuses and exploitation in the sex industry can to a large extent be attributed to existing regulatory frameworks around prostitution specifically, but also around sexuality and mobility in general. The large variety of ways in which states regulate prostitution can be simplified into three major models. These are the prohibitionist model, which criminalises all prostitution-related activities; the abolitionist model, which does not penalise prostitution per se but does repress any economic exploitation of the prostitution by others; and finally the regulationist model, which recognises prostitution as a profession and a legitimate sphere of market activity. For the latter, states' criminalisation of prostitution is seen as major reason why some sex workers work in exploitative, degrading or dangerous conditions, or suffer harassment from police and clients. As a way of improving prostitutes' working conditions, minimising the level of violence and gaining access to employment and citizenship rights, this strand of feminism and sex workers' activism advocates the legalisation of prostitution.

The Netherlands was the first country in Europe to legalise prostitution. In October 2000, the Dutch Parliament removed consensual adult prostitution from the criminal code, and acknowledged prostitution as a commercial activity subject to the same labour regulations and occupational guidelines as any other sector. Undocumented migrant sex workers, however, did not experience an improvement of their working conditions or gain entitlement to rights. Rather, the legalisation of prostitution resulted in undocumented migrant workers leaving the Netherlands or in them being pushed further underground when the 'zones of tolerance' within which they predominantly worked, were shut down by municipal authorities. The legalisation of prostitution did not, therefore, necessarily lessen the exploitation that workers experience in the sex sector or bring about in equal measure an improvement of prostitutes' working lives. While the legal situation of undocumented migrant workers did not change with the legalisation of prostitution, what did change and is novel in the regulation of the sex sector is that the law drew a line between sex workers on the basis on their nationality. In legalising the work of EU nationals while keeping the work of non-EU nations illegal, the sex sector followed the larger pattern of opening up markets and labour in Europe to the EU citizens and severely restricting the labour mobility of non-EU citizens.

The causes of abuse and exploitation of migrants in the sex sector are commonly attributed to 'traffickers' or individual 'evildoers'. In recent times, in the UK, public and media attention have been increasingly directed towards employers and pimps who keep migrant workers in conditions akin to slavery, deny them freedom to move and change work and prevent their access to basic social rights such as hospital treatment. These concerns follow from the stories of criminal Mafia-like groups that supply young women for forced labour in the sex sector by abducting or deceiving them through a false work promise. While I do not dispute that some third parties use force in order to pressure women to migrate and work in the sex sector, I relate a very different story about the role of immigration and employment regulations in the EU in producing and sustaining the conditions that permit migrants' exploitation in the sex sector. To put this simply: if third parties control-ling migrants' labour were not denying them labour mobility or access to the basic social rights, the state would.

This book does not embrace the narrative of (women as) victims of (men's) criminal doing or of poverty and economic deprivation but instead works through and offers a nuanced reading of structural fac-tors and social locations that inform a desire and decision to move as well as influence the mode and means by which these get acted out. Additionally, this book does not consign migrant labour in the sex sector to the idea of slavery but unpacks the working arrangements in third party controlled prostitution to show that conditions of confine-ment are maintained though a combination of factors such as third party control, the power state exercises over undocumented migrants, and migrant women's individual circumstances. Far from saying that migrant women in the sex sector do not suffer abuse, violence or exploitation – because as this study shows they often do – what I am contending is that abusive working arrangements in the sex sector are not permanent or monolithic but open to negotiation and change over time depending on a shifting set of relationship between clients, police, peer workers, women and third parties. It is certainly impossible to make sense of why people migrate and work in exploitative labour con-ditions in the sex sector without paying attention to economic factors and financial need. A key issue that this book brings to the fore, how-ever, is that an economic rationale alone is not sufficient to understand the intricacy of migrant lives and needs to be complemented with an analysis of emotional investments and by the hold gender difference exercises upon subjects. In this respect, apparently insignificant factors such as migrant women's beliefs about femininity and sexuality can play a key role in their entering, continuing or quitting work in the sex sector.

At the core of this book are the experiences and narratives of women from eastern European non-EU states who migrated to Italy and worked in third party controlled street prostitution. In the chapters that follow, I show that the complexity of desires and decisions behind women's migratory projects, the interdependency of structural and personal forces that sustained the conditions of exploitation and the multiple social positions and identification that women took up in relation to prostitution get simplified or, worse, obfuscated when an attempt is made to account for them under the rubric of 'trafficking' in women. By grounding my analysis in women's subjectivities and undertaking a detailed investigation of women's migratory projects, cross-border journeys and working arrangements with third parties, and the tensions that arise from women's attempts to identify themselves as victims, I aim to bring to the fore the relationship between the enactment of mobility at the 'micro' level and its unequal distribution at the 'macro' level. I shall argue that trafficking discourse and anti-trafficking policies sustain and normalise a differential regime of mobility through which the EU hierarchically organises access to its labour market and citizenship. With its emphasis on criminal organisations and victimised women, the discourse on sex trafficking as the new slave trade depoliticises the debate on migration and labour and closes down the possibility for seeing the ways in which women's assertion of social positions, that are not deemed legitimate for victims of 'sex trafficking', press onto and reshape the boundaries of citizenship in Europe.

Globalisation, mutations in labour relations and cross-border flows

The present changes in economy, labour markets and labour relations have been addressed by the abundant literature on globalisation. These works have examined the internationalisation of the financial markets and the consequent crisis of the welfare state in the Western world and of the nationally regulated labour systems. Much attention has been paid to the delocalisation of production from the Western world to regions where production and labour costs are considerably lower, and to the formation of an integrated and complex global system of production and exchange. With the rise of post-industrialism, the emergence of the service economy and deindustrialisation profound changes have taken place regarding work and employment relations. The closure of traditional industrial and serial production due to deindustrialisation brought about massive redundancies of workers. In eastern Europe in the context of 'transition' from the planned to market economy and the loss of state-guaranteed services and welfare this was felt even more acutely. The difficulty of re-entering the production process and the shift in that process towards 'immaterial' labour, labelled as such due to the increasing subjective, affective, relational and communicative quality of work, resulted in insecure and flexible employment relations well captured by the terms 'precarity' and 'precarious labour'.

Often used to describe these transformations, the references to 'feminisation of work' and 'becoming-woman of production' (Precarias a la Deriva, 2004) suggest that this model of labour incorporates as central the type of work previously undervalued and delegated to women under the heading of 'reproductive labour'. Consequently, this entails that the gendered division of labour organised around the distinction between reproductive and productive labour and the private and public sphere, typical of what used to be the Fordist mode of production, has changed too due to the fact that the capital is no longer able to exploit this distinction as a means of creating value (Papadopoulos et al., 2008; Marazzi, 2007). This does not imply that the dualism of production/ reproduction no longer exists, but rather that reading it exclusively in terms of a gendered division of labour does not fully capture contemporary forms of labour arrangements. Feminist scholars have made an important contribution to mapping out the new emerging configurations of intimate life and emotional labour. For example, feminist sociologist Arlie Hochshild (1997, 1983) has shown though the analysis of customer-oriented relational work that the transformations of the private and public domains are resulting in the transposition of emotional labour from the sphere of domesticity to that of commerce.

Some of the most interesting work in this field is taking place in studies of the sex industry. Elizabeth Bernstein's (2007) research on sex work in North America and western Europe links the transformations in the global economy to the shifts in the erotic and intimate sphere. She shows that the redrawing of the boundaries between public and private life and intimacy and commerce has transformed sex work to such an extent that sexual commerce, in these post-industrial contexts, is no longer grounded in its opposition to the private sphere but is invested by the emotional and affective labour once associated with the intimate or domestic. Bernstein coins the term 'bounded authenticity' to suggest that what is being sold and purchased is the authentic emotional and physical connection and to indicate that at the same time this exchange is emotionally bounded. Similarly, Amalia Cabezas (2004) uses the lens of tourism and sexual commerce in Cuba to examine how the creation of seasonal work, diversification of informal market arrangements and the wearing away of the boundaries between the formal and informal economy have led to the flexible reorganisation of the labour process. She in particular shows how the sphere of intimacy and sexuality plays into the reorganisation of labour as well as into the new models of social organisation of the personal romance (Cabezas, 2004).

These studies of sex commerce from the perspective of flexibilisation of labour and mutations in intimate life have developed alongside feminist research on the increase of sex tourism and the sex industry globally as consequences of globalisation and the rise of the service sector more generally. This strand of research focuses on the gendered effects of globalisation, in particular in South East Asia and the former Soviet Union and eastern Europe (Kligman and Limoncelli, 2005) and sees sex tourism and sex trafficking chiefly as consequences of rural impoverishment, urban unemployment and women's economic vulnerability and low social status, all engendered by the restructuring of the economy (Samarasinghe, 2008; Pettman, 1997; Troung, 1990). Global processes then, as Ursula Biemann (2002: 76), a filmmaker and scholar working on globalisation and the sex trade, has put it, 'address women directly in their sexuality' and need to be seen not as side effects of the 'formal' economy but rather as its structural part.

The position of women in the global economy had been interpreted as that of marginalisation in the low-wage sectors in the export assembly plants (Nash, 2006; Wright, 2006) or in the service sector in the advanced capitalist economies (Hondagneu-Sotelo, 2001; Anderson, 2000). Italy is rather interesting in this respect. On the one hand, as an EU member state, it has undergone integration and deregulation of its market as part of the EU integration process and, on the other hand, as a Southern European country, it features a large informal economy driven by irregular employment and constituted of a flexible labour force. This 'flexibilisation' has had an effect on the segmentation of the labour market on the basis of gender, age, nationality and race, and on the consequent emerging of the market 'niches' such as agriculture or the sex industry (Anthias and Lazaridis, 2000). The demand for low-wage labour in the service sector, which is both gendered and racialised, encourages women's migration and represents an alternative economic global circuit, despite its concentration in the service and 'informal' economies such as domestic, care and sex sectors. Saskia Sassen identifies cross-border migration, trafficking for the sex industry and the development of various types of formal and informal labour markets in terms of 'counter-geographies' of globalisation due to their growth in importance as profit-making activities for the actors partaking in them such as migrant women, agents/contractors and the governments of departure countries (Sassen, 2000).

Agents/contractors feature as central to a large body of scholarship on 'sex trafficking' that approaches the issue from the perspective of organised crime. Much of this scholarship is policy oriented and attempts to answer such questions as how criminal organisations operate, what are their type, size, and structure, and what governments ought to do in order to combat criminal networks. In this respect, this strand of scholarship works within the logic of the United Nations *Protocol to Suppress and Punish Trafficking in Persons, Especially Women and Children*, developed by the UN Crime Commission as a supplement to the *Convention Against Transnational Organized Crime*.[1] Adopted in November 2000 and entered into force in December 2003, the Protocol is an instrument of international cooperation aimed at developing a new international legal regime geared towards strengthening state cooperation in combating transnational organised crime. It sets out a number of measures to be adopted by the states in order to enhance law enforcement, improve information exchange and develop international cooperation among law enforcement agencies. For trafficking to be legally acknowledged, the three-elements chain, namely, the act (or recruitment, transportation), the means to enforce the act (threat, use of force) and the outcome (exploitation), need to be present. The Convention distinguished trafficking from smuggling, standing for facilitation and profiting from consensual, albeit 'illegal', movement of persons across borders.[2] The two definitions thus rely on a neat separation between involuntary and non-consensual (i.e. trafficking) and voluntary and consensual (i.e. smuggling) processes of migration. Trafficking stands for an involuntary and non-consensual process in which traffickers recruit and transport a person with the purpose of exploiting his/her labour on destination. Smuggling on the other hand is a voluntary and consensual form of migration in which the smuggler's role is restricted to the facilitation of irregular border crossing. Both are categories under the rubric of organised crime.

The increase in criminal activities in connection with cross-border migration and the expansion of criminal networks have been attributed to the global commodification of the migration process and the demand for illegal workers (Kyle and Koslowski, 2001). These studies commonly identify 'sex trafficking' as one of the fastest growing areas of criminal activity and, following trade in drugs and weapons, the third largest source of profits for organised crime (Miko, 2003). Scholars disagree on the involvement and role of organised criminal networks in cross-border migration. Some ascribe a key role to large transnational criminal syndicates such as the Russian Mafia (Aronowitz, 2009; Ebbe, 2008; Caldwell et al., 1999), while others argue that 'traffickers' are more likely to be smaller criminal groups or corrupt individuals and entre-preneurs (Finckenauer and Schrock, 2003; Bruinsma and Meershoek, 1999). The field of these studies is constituted mainly by two aspects of organised crime: the degree of influence exercised by certain members of the network over others; and the degree of coordination. The focus here is on the specialisation and division of tasks and social relation-ship, meaning whether and how the members are related to each other (whether by ethnic, familiar or friendship bonds).

Similarly to the studies that approach sex markets from the perspective of globalisation, this strand of scholarship looks at the diversification of criminal networks, the proliferation of criminal activities and the transnational profile of these networks. The aim is to show how these need to be viewed as separate from traditional organised crimes groups such as the Italian Mafia, which is organised hierarchically and managed centrally (Monzini, 2005). Researchers on 'trafficking' for the sex indus-try in Europe have differentiated between three main types of criminal networks: Albanian, post-Soviet and Balkan. The Albanian type involves closed ethnic networks, which are small and loosely connected and in which recruitment, transport and exploitation are handled by the same individuals that draw profit from supplying and transferring of women internationally. The post-Soviet model features networks of employment agencies encompassing several countries but managed by a culturally homogeneous group. This type is also referred to as a 'natural resource model' due to the fact the business is organised around recruitment of women who are said to be as widely available as natural resources such as timber (Leman and Janssens, 2008). The post-Soviet model also integrates Balkan groups, which serve as middlemen. This model is identified as Balkan Crime Groups and singled out as opportunistic, highly profitable and characterised by a high level of violence against women (Aronowitz, 2009). The research also shows that these models are undergoing significant changes and developing towards so-called multi-ethnic joint ventures; namely businesses with transnational pro-file with 'traffickers' adjusting to the working of the market and adapting their operations to the existing demand for forced labour (Leman and Janssens, 2008).

Elaborating on these studies but also departing from them, it is my claim in this book that a perspective on 'sex trafficking' as a form of organised crime or as a poverty-driven consequence of economic restructuring stabilises the ongoing changes in labour relations, citizenship and state sovereignty in Europe though a stereotypical and yet familiar and reassuring gendered framework. This shows clearly in anti-trafficking campaigns across eastern Europe, which equate women's informal labour migration with forced prostitution and indirectly encourage women to stay at home (I discuss these campaigns in Chapter 5). By doing so, the campaigns place images of migrant women within traditional representations of womanhood, and within a gendered division of labour that positions women outside of the labour market ('production') and inside the realm of the home ('reproduction'). So whereas EU citizens are encouraged to undertake greater labour mobility, anti-trafficking campaigns intervene upon the labour mobility of female non-EU nationals and encourage them to remain at home.

Citizenship rights across countries in the EU, primarily activated through practices of free movement, are first and foremost granted to citizens of member states and only partially or differentially extended to citizens of the so-called accession countries and to third-country nationals. EU citizens of the 'old Member States' enjoy complete freedom of movement, including labour mobility. A8 nationals,[3] who have access to the labour market of some but not all EU member states, will gain full labour mobility in 2011,[4] whereas the access of A2 nationals[5] to the EU labour market is restricted until 2013. Non-EU nationals, also referred to as third-country nationals, who are not already residents in one of the EU member states, have no right to free movement and are subjected to visa requirements and labour quotas. While I will expand on this differentiation in Chapter 5, at this point I put forward the claim that to look at 'sex trafficking' through the lens of mobility exposes the increasing impact of market logic on citizenship, and a consequent proliferation of different forms of citizenship. In saying this, I do not mean to offer an uncritical praise of the neoliberal reforms that introduce market arrangements into social and political life, but rather to suggest that instead of the straightforward exclusion of migrants from citizenship, as argued in some of the literature on migration discussed earlier, we are witnessing the differentiation and stratification of legal statuses and citizenship in the EU. That gender and sexuality are crucial in order to understand this dynamic is well exemplified by the fact that A8 nationals can work as self-employed sex workers in the Netherlands and yet, at the same time and irrespective of citizenship status, sex workers are disqualified from fully exercising freedom of movement as when for example subjected to the Anti-Social Behaviour Orders in the United Kingdom (ICRSE, 2005: 3).

In advancing these claims, I build and expand on the critical body of scholarship in social sciences that approached 'trafficking' for the sex and other sectors from the perspective of migration and labour. These works have as their focus the working of the labour markets and the demand for migrant labour, in particular 'trafficked' labour for the sex industry. They show that far from being simply a matter of 'pull' and 'push' market forces or a result of a criminal intervention, the demand for trafficked labour for the sex sector is produced by a combination of economic, social and political factors and mediated by residency and employment regulations in the destination states (Mai, 2009b; Anderson and O'Connell Davidson, 2003). Studies of 'trafficking' related to labour markets, as the one conducted by Bridget Anderson, demonstrate the need to interrogate the role of residency and employment regulations in creating marginalised groups without access to the formal labour market whose low-waged labour is permitted and sought by employers (Anderson, 2007). In turn, scholars have raised the question of whether is it possible at all to distinguish 'trafficking' from other forms of abuse and exploitation of migrant labour or to draw a line between forced and free labour (O'Connell Davidson, 2010; Rogaly, 2008).

These considerations have been extended to those perspectives that see 'trafficking' as an outcome of criminals' purposeful action at the departure and geared towards migrants' labour exploitation on arrival. Empirical studies of how and through whom women migrated show that people involved in organising women's travel in their countries of origin might not be the same that accompany them during the travel or exploit their labour in the destination countries. These activities might but do not need to be connected or managed by the same network of agents (Orfano, 2003; Wijers and Lap-Chew, 1997). Scholars have further pointed to the need to examine the association of trafficking with organised crime in its historical and political specificity. This means, as the work of Claudia Aradau (2008) shows, that trafficking is not simply a descriptive but rather a political category. Governments, by linking trafficking to organised crime, could identify trafficking as a threat to national security and pursue a securitarian agenda.

There is a disproportion between the imaginary of the organised crime as a large overarching structure, and the fact that the UN Convention Against Transnational Organised Crime, of which the Trafficking Protocol is a part, defines an organised criminal group as 'a structured group of three or more persons'.[6] For his part, Dag Stenvoll (2002) asks us to reflect on how the studies that uncritically identify organised crime with post-Soviet networks or with the Russian Mafia foster common

assumptions about large-scale criminalisation of eastern European societies in the post-1989 period and fuel the fear of a westward expansion
of criminal networks. As 'sex trafficking' gained visibility and political
urgency in the post-1989 years, when Europe at large was being transformed by a series of political revolutions in eastern Europe as well as by
the EU's unification, integration and enlargement, we must ask to what
extent the discourse of 'sex trafficking' as organised crime reflects anxieties about the ongoing political, economic and social changes in Europe
(Berman, 2003).

When attention is paid to the thinking and planning women put into
migrating and their description of the type, role and input of agents who
assisted them in organising their travel or brought them to the EU, we
are urged to rethink and question the neat separation between involuntary and voluntary processes of migration set out by the trafficking and
smuggling UN Protocols. The descriptions of the working arrangements
in sex work and of the type of jobs migrant women have taken up once
they left street prostitution, show that the conditions and confinement
in third party controlled prostitution are not maintained simply through
third party control. Just as important are residency and labour laws,
which, far from excluding migrant women from the labour market,
supply the conditions of possibility for their inclusion as flexible,
exploitable, and 'illegal' labour (Andrijasevic, 2009). What women's
experiences of migration and labour in the sex industry show us, therefore, is that the discourse of 'sex trafficking' as organised crime or forced
labour is intrinsically linked to the reorganisation of European citizenship and to its hierarchical organisation via a differential as well as a
gendered and sexually coded distribution of labour mobility.

Migration, sex work and feminist inquiry

Feminist migration scholars have played a key role in developing analyses
of migratory flows that challenge the mainstream view of labour migration as being male-driven. They have shown women's past and present
active roles as primary migrants and revealed the normative impact of
heterosexuality and the nuclear family on immigration laws. Throughout
the 1980s, immigration regulations in several European countries upheld
a gendered division of labour by assigning women a 'dependent' status
that kept many migrant women out of paid employment. This was done
through family reunification schemes, which assumed that the man was
the economically motivated migrant actor, the 'breadwinner', and the
woman was his dependent (Bosniak, 2007; Morokvasic, 1984).

Theories of migratory flows that postulate men as 'primary' and women as 'secondary' migrants universalise a rather specific model, namely that of the guest–worker during the mass labour migration in Europe between the 1950s and mid-1970s. This model, developed by Bohning (1984), is organised around the idea of distinct stages where the migratory process is initiated by single young men, and followed by older married men who are joined at a later stage by their spouses and children as a way of supplementing household income (Kofman et al., 2000). This simplistic conceptualisation of migratory processes rests on the classical dualism that identifies the male with activity, production and the public sphere, and female subjectivity with passivity, reproduction and the private sphere, and it heavily influenced migrant women's positions as dependents with derived rights and their exclusion from citizenship (Walsum and Spijkerboer, 2007).[7]

Today, while formal immigration laws have changed so that in the EU migrant men and women have equal rights to family reunification, the gendered and racialised coding of the labour markets still impacts differently on women and men. Migrant women often work in sectors of the economy such as in domestic and caring work, where the temporality or informality of employment relations, the level of income and the type of living arrangements make it difficult to satisfy the requirements of family reunification. The right of women who are EU nationals to reside with a non-EU husband and establish a family in the wife's country of citizenship is still questioned in a way that the right of male EU citizens is not. A review of European legal decisions has shown that in cases when non-EU nationals are refused a residence permit or are under threat of deportation, national courts expect the wife to follow the husband to his country of citizenship, even in cases when the wife is a white EU citizen (de Hart, 2007). In short, women and men still stand in a different relationship to citizenship, usually to the disadvantage of women (Lister, 2004).

Given feminists scholarship's pivotal contribution in placing women and gender firmly on the migration research agenda, and in offering a more complex view of contemporary migration by examining women's active participation in migratory processes, I've found it surprising that feminist migration scholars, who invested so much theoretical and political work in making visible women's role as active migrants rather than passive victims, did not extend this line of analysis to 'sex trafficking'. For example, in her analysis of 'sex trafficking' in Greece, Gabriella Lazaridis posits the situation of migrant women in the Greek sex industry as that of a series of overlapping exclusions caused by economic restructuring and the decline in the status of women in eastern Europe and the former Soviet

Union, the manipulation of organised crime, the confinement and exploitation of women and Greek society's sexist and racist attitudes towards migrant women. These multiple forms of exclusion and the impossibility to escape the spaces of marginalisation result in the reduction of women's opportunities in life, loss of identity and control over their lives and consequently in women's position of slaves (Lazaridis, 2001).

Similarly, in their overview of 'sex trafficking' and sex work debates, the authors of *Gender and International Migration in Europe* do not acknowledge the migratory project or agency of migrant women in the sex industry or the complexity of working arrangements in third party controlled prostitution. While explicitly distancing themselves from the term 'victim', the portrayal they offer of 'trafficked' women as not getting paid, deceived about the type of work, deprived of their passports, and held in captivity by third parties, and the slippage they make between adult sex work and the commercial sexual exploitation of children, nevertheless come very close to the image of a victim (Kofman et al., 2000). Mirjana Morokvasic's key contribution on East-to-West women's migration in Europe continues this trend when she contrasts the newly acquired labour mobility and opportunities for eastern European women in the post-1989 period to the lack of mobility and freedom for 'trafficked' women. As eastern Europeans are now 'free to leave and come back', short-term labour mobility has become a 'lifestyle', a source of empowerment and a new opportunity for most – except for trafficked women, whose mobility and existence are posited as totally dependent on 'traffickers' (Morokvasic, 2004).

After doing research for more than ten years on the issue of 'sex trafficking', I am still uncertain why many feminist migration scholars, whose work has been groundbreaking in advancing a gendered reading of the migratory flows and of women as primary migrants, fail to extend this type of analysis to 'sex-trafficking'. This failure exists despite a slow but steady proliferation of empirical studies problematising the view of migrant women in the sex industry as involuntary migrants, and illustrating the degree of agency migrant women working in indoor and outdoor prostitution exercise despite the restrictions imposed on their labour and mobility (Gülçür and İlkkaracan, 2002; Brussa, 2002; Thorbek and Pattanaik, 2002; McDonald et al., 2000).

The difficulty in thinking of migrant women in the sex sector as active migrants, or of 'sex trafficking' in terms of a governmental category geared towards control of migration, can also be found in certain parts of the feminist activist community in Europe. In 2006, the

NextGENDERation, a European network of feminist scholars and activists, brought to the European Social Forum (ESF) in Athens a discussion panel entitled 'What's Wrong with Current Anti-Trafficking Politics? A Migrants and Labour Rights Perspective for a New European Agenda'. I was one of the coordinators and speakers on the panel and our aim was to intervene in the feminist discussion on 'sex trafficking' and shift the terms of the debate from violence against women and organised crime towards that of migration and labour, in order to avoid women's migration and participation in the sex industry being reduced to the notion of sexual slavery.[8] Even though the panel was well received and attended by several hundred activists, NextGENDERation was unsuccessful in having it accepted under the feminist axis. It was held as part of the migration axis, since the take on 'sex trafficking' NextGENDERation was putting forward was deemed incompatible with the ESF feminist agenda by the organising committee. While having the seminar under the migration axis turned out to be analytically and politically rewarding, the impossibility of having the panel included under the feminist axis illustrates well the obstacles to opening up a migration and labour perspective on sex work in women's groups that are part of social movements in Europe.

This episode in which the NextGENDERation was prohibited to partake in the feminist axis is best understood in the context of the strand of feminism that conceives of prostitution in terms of men's violence against women. Developed by radical feminists usually referred to as 'abolitionists', this stands by the position that prostitution needs to be understood in relation to the body and consequently the self. Since in this case sexuality is equated with intimacy and seen as inherently private, this stand of feminism identifies prostitution with selling of the self and hence as a self-estranging activity 'destructive of woman's humanity' (Barry, 1995: 32). Prostitution therefore constitutes an act of objectification of women's bodies that reinforces patriarchal structure of domination (MacKinnon, 1989). Abolitionists see men's sexuality as violent, dominant and functional to maintaining patriarchal power. When this reasoning is extended to 'trafficking', clients and 'traffickers' (both understood exclusively as male), as well as patriarchal social relations in migrant prostitutes' (understood exclusively as female) countries of origin, are seen as principal causes of 'trafficking'. The latter is moreover interpreted as emblematic of a patriarchal social order that governs gender arrangements in women's countries of origins. 'Trafficking' thus becomes a matter of supply and demand: it is brought about by the low status of women and is sustained by clients' demand for prostitution (Jeffreys, 1997). Given the fact that prostitution reduces women to bought objects, there can be no distinction between 'forced' and 'free choice' prostitution, since it will always and necessarily be degrading and damaging to women.[9] As Carol Wolkowitz puts it in her commentary of radical feminists' take on the body, radical feminists believe that prostitution results in a profound self-hate and that because the body of the prostitute has been de-selved and turned into an object she can no longer recognise its true interests and cannot be viewed as a subject who can speak for herself (Wolkowitz, 2006). The image of the prostitute put forward by the radical feminists is therefore that of a wounded woman who has no voice and whose injured body speaks for her (Doezema, 2001).

The assumption that women working in the sex sector cannot speak for themselves or access or make clear their interests and experiences is countered by feminists who adopt what might be termed a 'sex workers' rights' perspective. Sex workers' rights advocates have responded to the view of the prostitute as a passive victim by arguing that what is sold in prostitution is not the body but a service, and that what a client pays for is sex workers' time and not indiscriminate access to her body (Corso and Landi, 1998). They view sex work as a service sector job, and states' attempts to criminalise sex work or penalise sex workers as a denial of human rights to self determination to those who make an individual choice to enter prostitution. Positing sex work as a form of labour and an income-generating activity permits sex workers' rights advocates to contest claims that prostitution is invariably forced and degrading, and to emphasise instead that women choose sex work out of economic need and/or the feeling of control it gives them over sexual interactions (Delacoste and Alexander, 1988). It also allows for a critique of those positions that interpret prostitution as a form of psycho- or socio-pathological deviance of individual women. By pointing out the similarities between sex work and other types of labour, sex workers' rights advocates have tried to re-focus the attention onto the struggle for improving sex workers' rights and working conditions (Pheterson, 1996). I discuss the matter of 'trafficking' and sex work in more detail in Chapter 3, but want to say at this point that from the sex workers' rights perspective it is not men's demand for women's services or the existence of a market for commercial sex that leaves room for abuse and exploitation such as in the case of 'trafficking', but rather the lack of protection and labour rights for workers in the sex industry.

Agency and citizenship

In the literature, the debate between 'abolitionists' and sex workers' rights activists on prostitution is commonly referenced in terms of the contention over agency or lack thereof: while 'abolitionists' stress women in prostitution as victims of patriarchal oppression and domination, sex workers' rights activists stress women's agency in prostitution and argue that women in the sex industry are persons capable of making choices and decisions regarding their working and everyday lives. When viewed within the context of contemporary Europe and its ongoing social and political transformations, the feminist debate over prostitution has implications that go beyond the matter of agency. Instead, this contention speaks to the question of who is a legitimate political actor in the EU (Andrijasevic, Aradau, Huysmans, Squire, 2011). That the victim is a governmental category that delegitimates the political agency of certain groups of subjects (Aradau, 2004) is clearly visible in relation to the category of the 'victim of trafficking' (VoT) and in the ways in which it legally and discursively severely narrows certain groups capacity to act or make choices. We can observe this at work in the so-called Yani case when, in 1999, the Netherlands' Secretary of State for Justice denied residency permits to six self-employed prostitutes from Poland and the Czech Republic working in Amsterdam. Although it was later overruled by the European Court of Justice as in breach of the *Right of Establishment under the European Agreements* that gives nationals of the accession countries the right to free movement and self-employment in the EU, the Dutch state initially argued that women were not autonomous workers since it was impossible to establish whether they migrated and worked of their own free will.[10] Moreover, the fact that the main EU migration policy instrument on human trafficking – the so-called Trafficking Directive or, in full, the Council Directive for the 'short-term residence permit issued to victims of action to facilitate illegal migration or trafficking in human beings who co-operate with the competent authorities'[11] – identifies trafficking as a matter of illegal migration and classifies victims explicitly as third country nationals, shows the extent to which the category of the VoT needs to be examined for the role it plays in delimiting who can be an EU citizen.

What the category of the VoTs displaces from scrutiny is that European citizenship has been reorganised in such a way that it no longer follows a binary inclusion/exclusion model, but is rather characterised by the proliferation of citizenship statuses whereby that of illegality is just one among many statuses migrants hold over time (I discuss the apparent contradiction of illegality and citizenship further in Chapter 5). Additionally, we need to consider that the VoT might not be the best category to grasp the complexity and contradictions of the discourses and social practices constitutive of citizenship, in particular in relation to gender and sexuality, since it cannot account for the conflicts that arise from the formation of enlarged European space and citizenship via the regulation of labour mobility. The gendered migration perspective developed by feminist scholars of migration is useful here, because it brings to the fore migrant women's subjective desires for social, economic and affective mobility that inform their migratory projects. It also points to the struggles and efforts migrant women put into realising those desires and in dealing with hindrances to their mobility whether imposed through border control and visa or residency requirements or through third party control of their labour in prostitution.

Building on the critical feminist scholarship that contributed to making visible the migratory agency of women in the sex sector otherwise concealed by the rhetoric of victims and sexual slavery (Augustin, 2007; Kapur, 2004; Sharma, 2003), and in investigating in a nitty-gritty way the mode, length, frequency, itinerary and conditions of women's cross-border travel, I will show that women's migratory histories, motivations for migrating and the ways and means by which they reached Italy are similar and cannot be marked off clearly from other forms of women's labour migration. Given this consideration and the difficulty discussed in the previous section to distinguish between forced labour and other labour relations in which migrant workers are involved, I will attempt to avoid the use of the word 'trafficking' and speak instead of conditions of confinement or third party controlled prostitution to discuss the extent of unfreedom and exploitation migrant women suffered. When I employ the words 'trafficking' and VoTs, I do so to refer to these terms as they are defined by conventions, policies and legal instruments. When I put these terms in inverted comas, I do so to point to the limitations of this terminology and suggest that the situations referenced could be better described through a different term, such as illegality, vulnerability, exploitation or use of force.

The detailed discussion of women's migratory projects and cross-border travel, as well as of the negotiations they engage in and the relationships they develop aims to illustrate the capacity to act and respond to the oppressive conditions in third party controlled migrant street prostitution commonly understood in the literature on sex work as the sector where women suffer violence and abuse the most. When I speak of agency, therefore, I refer to the ways in which migrant women responded to, negotiated or failed to negotiate the restrictions imposed on their mobility by the social and legal position they occupied and by the relations of power through which these were sustained. This book extends, however, the analysis of agency to that of subjectivity and subjectivation. This entails a methodological and analytical shift from considering women's narratives as mere reflections of their experiences or testimonial recording of their voices, to approaching the narratives as sites of subject's formation.

Hence, the centrepieces of this book are women's narratives and subjectivities. This approach draws upon feminist standpoint theory, which argues that looking at the world from the perspective of women's lives generates new insights into the complexity of the social world and functions as a critique of dominant knowledge claims. Standpoint epistemologies engage and alter the conceptual schemes upon which the dominant knowledge claims are based (Harding, 1991). In extending the analysis to investigations of subjectivity, this book moves beyond reading agency in terms of antagonism to dominant structures and examines how individuals are multiply constituted subjects who take up a range of subject positions, some of which are contradictory and conflicting. Such an approach has been facilitated by social theorists' critique of the unified rational subject and the deployment of a nuanced concept of multi-layered subjectivity. Feminist scholars in particular have studied the construction of subjects in relation to both oppressive and affirmative power dynamics, advanced a nuanced discussion about how norms and discourses are inhabited, and investigated the role that fantasy, desire and unconscious investments play in the process of subject construction (Moore, 2007; Mahmood, 2005).

Informed by these theories, I make visible the tensions that emerge when migrant women in the sex sector take up several and contradictory subject positions. The case of Italy is extremely interesting in this respect because Italy is the only country in Europe that grants a renewable residence and work permit to VoTs. While much has been written about this law in terms of it being the best practice of victim protection (Pearson, 2002), what scholars have not yet addressed is the fact that the legal status of a trafficking victim is not simply bestowed on individuals but must be claimed actively through reference to specific patterns of violence and through a willingness to forego sex work. I show that paying attention to how women negotiate contradictory subject positions such as that of an 'active' migrant, a 'passive' victim and a 'money-earning' sex worker and to *what* makes women identify with and resist certain subject positions, permits us to see that the subject is processually constituted through several positionings. Migrant women's agency in the sex sector should, I contend, be examined in relation to both sex work and migration. Migration is lived or experienced differently by different subjects and cannot just be considered in the abstract.

In their being inherent in all aspects of a migratory project, gender and sexuality are crucial in order to understand this dynamic and must be taken into consideration when investigating contemporary migrant subjectivity. This entails paying attention to how gender and sexuality are taken up by the regulatory regimes but also, importantly, how gender and sexuality inform migrant women's and men's investments in the migratory project in terms of femininity and masculinity (Mai, 2009a). When migrant women in third party controlled street prostitution take up and assert conflicting subject positions that cannot be accommodated by the category of the VoT, we are witnessing a rupture in formal and commonly accepted conceptualisations of European citizens and women. In their multiple identifications and in enacting mobility despite restrictions imposed on the movement of third-country nationals, criminalisation of sex work and its exclusion from the free movement of labour and services, migrant women destabilise the defining features of the category of femininity and that of citizenship by illustrating the key role non-citizens play in a remaking of the public and private spheres, rearranging of the markets and labour relations and in interrupting the logic of the political rooted in the dichotomous forms of belonging.

Fieldwork and interviews

This book is embedded in and organised around the narratives of migrant women from eastern European non-EU member states whose arrival in Italy was facilitated and managed by third parties, both individuals and agencies. They all worked in street prostitution under different degrees of confinement and in conditions of economic exploitation by one or more third parties. Italy presents a unique field of study on this topic since it is the only EU state to include in its immigration law a clause that allows for the social protection and legalisation of trafficking victims. In 1999 and 2000, I conducted fieldwork in Bologna, the city that, for over a decade, has featured innovative projects on 'trafficking' such as the outreach street project *Moonlight*, and *Progetto Delta*, the latter focused on social protection and/or voluntary repatriation of 'trafficking victims'. I conducted fieldwork at *Casa delle donne per non subire violenza* or Women's Shelter in Bologna part of the Progetto Delta. As part of the fieldwork I also worked at the shelter as a 'social worker'[12] in the project that offered housing and legal assistance to migrant women who left street prostitution. Working as a consultant was not new to me. I had previously worked in the very same project in

1995 and 1996, the period when I first became interested in the topic of 'trafficking'. Working in the Women's Shelter provided me with access to migrant women who have exited prostitution and were hosted by the shelter while deciding whether to return to their countries of origin or stay in Italy. Since some of the women had been with the shelter for several months when I met them, I had the possibility of following their process of legalisation and what it meant to them. Conducting interviews in the period that followed women's exit from street prostitution and being present while they were attempting to find housing or work offered unique insights into the difficulties women faced upon exiting sex work.

I collected accounts of 30 migrant women and conducted unstructured in-depth interviews with 15 of them. In the in-depth interviews, which consisted of unstructured open-ended questions about the life history of the subjects, women told their stories of migration, work in street prostitution, community relations and settlement in Italy. All of the interviews were taped, fully transcribed and ranged from one-and-a-half to three hours in length. The difference between total numbers of women spoken to and interviewed is due to a number of factors. If, after having exited third party controlled street prostitution, migrant women decided to return to their countries of origin, there was materially no time to conduct an interview with them. Most of their days were occupied by police interrogation, medical checks and the arrangement of travel documents. Language often represented a barrier in conducting interviews since I needed to arrange for a translator from Russian, Romanian or Moldovian languages. The lack of time and the difficulty of communicating also made it hard to establish a relationship of trust with a number of women and thus limited the amount of in-depth interviews. Given these factors, the 15 interviews were conducted with two groups of women. First, with women who, after exiting street prostitution and before returning home, stayed in Italy for several weeks. Second, with women who decided to stay in Italy and were busy arranging their permanence. This longer span of time allowed me to build a relationship of trust with these women and conduct the interviews in Italian, which was spoken by most of the respondents who stayed in Italy.

Interviewing migrant women in the sex industry can be particularly difficult when they work in situations of control and confinement imposed upon them by third parties. Until recently, interviews with 'trafficked' women did not feature among the scholarly literature on 'sex trafficking' in Europe. The difficulty of gathering women's narratives can result in paradoxical and methodologically quite problematic situations. For example, when the Stichting Tegen Vrouwenhandel (STV),[13] the main (feminist) NGO working on assisting 'trafficked victims' and the sole organisation with centralised data on 'trafficked' women in the Netherlands, stepped out from a major EU-sponsored study on trafficking in women, the two researchers were faced with a lack of data and the impossibility of accessing the target group (Payoke et al., 2003). In order to conduct the study, the researchers resorted to police channels and gained access to five so-called reception centres where VoTs, along with other undocumented migrants, were detained. This resulted in a paradoxical situation in which, while being detailed and awaiting the decision whether they will be allowed to stay in the Netherlands or deported to their countries of origin, women were interviewed about the ways they had reached the country (see Hopkins and Nijboer, 2003). This situation is methodologically problematic because if women failed to present themselves as victims of severe exploitation and in need of state protection, they could have jeopardised their already slim chances of being granted the right to stay in the Netherlands as trafficking victims.

As in other research situations where studies were based on interviews with 'trafficked' women (see Payoke et al., 2003; Maluccelli, 2001; Carchedi et al., 2000), my access to the respondents was mediated by an NGO, namely by the Bologna Women's Shelter. While working at the shelter provided me with 'access' to the group of women I wished to interview, it also imposed limits to my work, especially when it came to conducting in-depth interviews. Working as a 'social worker' at the shelter meant that at times I would conduct intake talks with migrant women who had just exited third party controlled prostitution. This meant reconstructing with them the story of how they reached Italy, discussing whether they preferred to return home or remain in Italy, looking into the possibilities of realising the option they preferred and finally arranging the formalities concerning their housing for the necessary period of time. Having done the intake talk with me, some women were puzzled and did not immediately understand the purpose of doing yet another interview. Additionally, the double role of a social worker and a researcher was on one occasion a ground for confusion that transformed a situation of a 'fieldwork-interview' into a 'social worker-consultation' session.

In order to reduce as much as possible the confusion of roles, I decided not to conduct in-depth interviews with women with whom I did intake talks. I also limited the intake talks to the initial period of my fieldwork during which I familiarised myself with the landscape in which women moved (i.e. their points of reference) and the vocabulary they used. For example, the women rarely, if ever, used the word 'prostitute'. Instead, they would refer to prostitution as 'the street', 'work' or just 'hmm'. Learning the vocabulary women used meant devoting space to participant-observation. This entailed visiting women at the places they lived; participating in women's daily activities such as shopping, cooking, informal chats; assisting them in looking for a job and handling matters with foreign police; helping out with Italian language, in particular when something needed to be put in written form; babysitting when necessary; hanging out in bars from time to time and, finally, being a source of information with regard to immigration procedures concerning travelling and working in EU countries other than Italy. In order to diversify the sample of women, I used the snowball method and approached women who were in the past assisted legally by the shelter but never lived in its facility, as well as those women who were not assisted by the shelter in any way.

The respondents

To safeguard the safety and privacy of the women I interviewed, all names have been altered and the dates on the legal documents, which could facilitate respondents' identifications, have been omitted. They were aged between 18 and 25, and originated from Croatia, Moldova, Romania, Ukraine and Russia. The common characteristic of these states is that, at the time, they were all non-EU member states, which allowed me to examine the ways and mode of women's cross-border migration. All respondents reached Italy through the assistance of third parties, whether individuals or agencies, but they got recruited differently and travelled different routes. I differentiated the sample so as to include respondents who migrated via individuals or agencies; those who travelled with or without valid documents; those who travelled at their own or on third party's expenses and those who travelled to Italy via Southern-Eastern route[14] as well as those who arrived via the Northern-Eastern route[15] (Orfano, 2003). I have also paid attention to interviewing women who migrated to Italy more than once. This was sometimes due to them being apprehended by the border police during the journey or deported after they have reached Italy, or to them returning to Italy for the second time to take up a sex work contract.

Upon their arrival in Italy all of the women worked in street prostitution under the control of one or more third parties. To have a more thorough picture of the working conditions in street prostitution, the sample includes women who have stayed in third party controlled prostitution for quite a short period of time, those who were controlled for a longer period, women who –when the third parties got arrested – stayed in street prostitution and worked on their own, and finally those who exited third party controlled prostitution and re-entered prostitution afterwards working independently. Paying attention to the length of stay in prostitution consented an analysis of the type of relationships women established in prostitution (e.g. with third parties, 'clients', police and with other migrant women), the conditions of confinement within prostitution and the resources women generated within the existing conditions of confinement.

In my choice of respondents I additionally paid attention to include those women who had decided to return to their countries of origin as well as those who had opted for remaining in Italy. Among the latter group I took into consideration the time factor and interviewed women who had been living in Italy for a period between five and fifteen months. This differentiation made it possible to explore how migrant women dealt with the stigma surrounding prostitution as well as how they experienced the process of legalisation and social protection devised for VoTs. This allowed me to see what type of jobs and labour contracts were available for migrant women who had exited sex work and were in possession of a residence and work permit.

Finally, it is important to reiterate that, at the time of the interviews, all of the respondents had already exited prostitution. Given the fact that my evidence, as well as other currently existing studies on 'trafficked' women in Europe are limited to this specific category of migrant women, it is difficult to know to what degree my results are representative of the larger population of women, or whether they are specific for a group of subjects who have already left prostitution. In order to establish the relevance of my data for a broader population of migrant women in prostitution, I have cross-referenced my results with studies on non-migrant street prostitution. My results point to the parallels between two situations and therefore question the presumed exceptionality of 'trafficked' women's conditions in street prostitution. I expand on this in detail in Chapter 3.

The structure of the book

This book investigates 'sex trafficking' from the perspective of migrant women's lives. This is best reflected in the organisation of the book as the three empirical chapters based on women's narratives constitute the centrepiece of the book.

Chapter 2 examines questions related to recruitment and travel and takes issue with the notions of deception, coercion and force as distinctive elements of 'trafficking'. In bringing into focus travel from departure to destination country and the episodes of border crossing, my analysis interrogates the criminalisation approach of states and examines the effects of immigration regulations on women's lives. I identify a gap between respondents' accounts of their migration and the dominant rhetoric of 'trafficking', and show how borders and border-controlling practices tend to enhance the vulnerability of migrants. The more difficult it is to migrate in a legal way, and the more irregular border crossings are made, the more dependent migrants are on agents and the more vulnerable they become to abuse and labour exploitation.

In Chapter 3, I investigate the conditions of control and confinement in street prostitution in Italy. My analysis differentiates between control exercised by third parties and economic and political structural forces that sustain the exploitation of migrant women's labour. I further discuss the relationships and resources women generated in order to regain their mobility and exit the conditions of confinement. I show that, over time, it was difficult for third parties to prevent migrant women from accumulating resources, such as personal networks, knowledge and money that made them more independent. Examples of migrant women involved as third parties, having done or still doing sex work themselves, disturb the picture of the sex worker/third party relationship as dichotomously gendered and unidirectionally exploitative.

Taking as its starting point the feminist debate on whether women are to be viewed as coerced victims or agents who choose sex work, Chapter 4 points to the limitations of such a perspective and proposes rethinking migration and prostitution as processes of subject's construction. This entails leaving space for the contradictions in women's narratives to emerge, and to investigate how the social positions women take up relate to their position as both migrants and sex workers. For instance, they had to deal with stigma, not only as prostitutes but sometimes also as 'Russian' or 'eastern European'. Many of the women did not tell partners, family and friends about their sex work, and felt that the danger of deportation and of anti-trafficking media campaigns was that they could be exposed as prostitutes and thus possibly be excluded from their communities of origin. Some of the women tried to rid themselves of stigma by portraying themselves as 'being forced' to sell sex out of an economic responsibility to their families. Relationships with Italian men were commonly seen as valuable, giving the women a more respectable status and bringing them closer to normative gender roles.

Embedding my findings within a larger body of scholarship on transformation of borders, labour and sovereignty, Chapter 5 shows that the discourses such as 'sex trafficking', 'sexual slavery' and 'victims of trafficking' are terrain where anxieties about change in Europe and contentions over entitlement to the European citizenship are played out. I discuss how migrant women's desire and the enactment of spatial, labour and social mobility needs to be seen in relation to the transformation of citizenship and polity in Europe that cannot be adequately grasped through dualisms such as inside/outside or citizens/aliens. In my concluding remarks I argue that the analytic models that privilege the notion of exclusion and see sex workers as paradigmatic examples of new forms of exclusions are inadequate for understanding the changing modes of governing and the emerging political subjectivities in Europe.

This book addresses various communities both inside and outside academia such as interdisciplinary migration specialists, sociologists, political scientists and policy scholars. To this end, I have positioned this book beyond the thresholds of academia, and deep into society. The choice of using women's narratives as a source of knowledge as well as engaging with the policy and legislative framework goes hand in hand with the work I have conducted during the last decade as an academic, activist and consultant on issues of 'sex trafficking', migration and citizenship in Europe. This book is written from a feminist perspective and aims to further the cause of feminism as an oppositional but also prepositional project capable of illuminating our understanding of power relations with great awareness of structural injustices and domination, but also with the determination to inspire alternative ways of knowledge and forms of action. To this end, I believe that feminist scholars should take the lead in making academic research more socially relevant. In today's world, scholars should, in my opinion, not be afraid of becoming more involved in both policymaking and social activism. Finally, I harbour the hope that the respondents whose lives inspired my work will find my modest contribution relevant and useful.

2
The Cross-Border Migration

'Do not ask us why we are here, ask us rather how we got here.'

Liudmila

Introduction

We will call them Olga and Natasha. Their story equals the stories of many other girls from the East who came to Italy blinded by a promise of work, and were then forced into prostitution by a pimp, a man of no scruples. As soon as they got off the bus that brought them illegally from Moldova to Italy, they were taken over by Rimi, an Albanian.[1]

In the style common to media stories of trafficking, the passage above from Bologna's daily newspaper speaks of unaware victims and preying criminals. This description goes hand in hand with the image of wide-scale deception and dispersal as the journalist infers that women are illegal migrants and compares the experiences of Olga and Natasha to that of many other women from eastern Europe. Whether it is journalistic, scholarly, governmental or non-governmental sources, reference to the large scale of 'trafficking' are deployed in order to stress the enormity of the problem and the urgency of combating it. The International Labour Organization (ILO) estimates that at least 2.45 million people have been trafficked globally between 1995 and 2004 into forced labour, including sexual exploitation (USDOS, 2009: 8). The US Department of State assesses this number to be between 600,000 and 800,000 each year (USDOS, 2006: 6). As for Europe, the UN Office on Drugs and Crime estimates that each year 250,000 women are trafficked in Europe for the sex sector (UNODC, 2009: 8).

And yet, far from being trustworthy these numbers are arbitrary and unreliable. The accuracy of these estimates came under question when the US Governmental Accountability Office (GAO) reviewed the numbers put forward by the US government and brought attention to methodological weaknesses, gaps in the data and numerical discrepancies. The GAO report criticised the US government's statistics for being compiled by a single person without evidence to back up the numbers, the impossibility to replicate the estimates and a large discrepancy between observed and estimated numbers of victims.[2] This discrepancy is best shown when the estimated numbers are compared to the data held by the International Organisation for Migration's (IOM) database on VoTs. The IOM data indicate that between 1999 and 2005 fewer than 8000 VoTs have been assisted by IOM missions in 26 countries (GAO, 2006: 12).

Whether one works with estimates or with the existing datasets, it is necessary to keep in mind that it is rather difficult to collect numerical data of VoTs due to the precarious and often irregular position of migrants, the situation of control under which they might be working, the fear and distrust they have towards the police and the divergent definitions of what constitutes 'trafficking'. However, what these numbers do show is that there is a large gap between estimated and real numbers and that much caution is needed when invoking tens of thousand of victims. As references to the magnitude of 'trafficking' are rarely backed up by the data and, when they are, they rely on questionable statistical estimates wherein numbers diverge by hundreds of thousands, there is a need for caution when referring to 'trafficking' being of 'epidemic proportions' (Pickup, 1998: 44) or on 'explosive increase' (Molina and Janssen, 1998: 16). Uncritical deployment of images of wide-scale deception misinterprets the reality of contemporary migratory movements by identifying women's migration for the sex sector with a 'very sad "slave trade" flourishing across Europe' (Orsini-Jones and Gatullo, 2000: 128) and all too easily feeds into moral panic surrounding migration and sex work.

In this chapter I examine what leads women to migrate and the ways in which they organise their travel and reach their destination. I am interested in bringing to the fore the plethora of factors and desires that inform women's migration to Italy and which remain obscured by the reference to the magnitude of sex 'trafficking' and the emphasis on use of coercion and deception as its key features. These posit mobility as a consequence of the forceful action of third parties or as an outcome of women's economic desperation. Against the tendency to reduce mobility to an imposition or to an economic logic, I look at the interaction between women and third parties, whether individual or agencies, who facilitated their travel and at non-economic factors such as gender-based violence or a desire for a romantic relationship that, as I show, are of no less importance in understanding women's migration than financial need. It is not abject poverty, brute force or sheer deceit that propel women to migrate and take up sex work, but rather the desire for economic, affective and geographic mobility. Migrant women's accounts of how, where, with whom and for how long they travelled before they arrived in Italy and their determination to pursue their projects undeterred show how restrictive visa policies and strict border controls produce conditions that exacerbate migrant women's vulnerability to abuse and exploitation.

What this chapter brings into focus then is the gap between women's accounts of how and why they migrated and the dominant rhetoric of trafficking. This discrepancy is particularly visible in the case of Olga and Natasha who, contrary to what the newspapers reported, were neither naïve nor deceived into prostitution. Rather, they returned to Italy for the second time to work again in street prostitution on a three-month contract but now for a different third party. They were also not illegal but in possession of passports and travelled on tourist visas. Women's accounts of their migration to Italy challenge the narrative of victims and organised crime and point to the need to take issues with the accepted notions of deception and coercion as constitutive of eastern European women's migration for sex work. I begin by tackling questions relative to the travel and 'recruitment' process and investigate respondents' cross-border movements. I suggest that the impact of border controls and visa policies on women's lives is a crucial element to be considered in the analysis of women's migration in Europe. In the final section of the chapter, I discuss how privileging poverty as the primary determinant of migration deflects the possibility of identifying the plethora of motives that inform women's migration and of seeing migrant women as complex subjects pursuing a desire to change their lives.

Past and present routes into migration

In the following sections I look at women's previous migratory experiences, examine the type of actors through which women organised and carried out their travel to Italy, and interrogate the notion of deception. These dispute a clear demarcation between voluntary and involuntary processes of migration and the subsequent inclusion of third party controlled sex work migration in the latter category.

Migratory histories

The concept of 'trafficking' conveys the impression of women's abrupt and unexpected departure caused through the intervention of third parties. This characterisation comes close to the idea of inexperienced and naïve women kidnapped by the 'traffickers'. That such representations are problematic is best visible when attention is paid to women's previous experiences of migration and to the time it took women to decide whether and how to leave for Italy. Most of the women, as I show in this section, had previous experience of labour migration or were familiar with women who migrated to work in restaurants or do domestic or sex work abroad. Some were unsuccessful in their attempts to migrate, got arrested and were deported before reaching Italy. Once they were returned home, they left again as 'home' was where they had started off from and where they did not want to be in the first place. As Larisa put it: 'After I returned home I didn't know what to do next ... all of those problems were there again.' A number of other women went to Italy twice, working each time in third party controlled street prostitution and returning home for a couple of months in between.

Some respondents previously lived and worked in countries other than Italy. Eugenia, for example, migrated from Romania to Serbia, where she found work as a waitress in a restaurant. Oksana migrated from Ukraine to Romania for seasonal agriculture work. Other women worked in the entertainment sector where some performed cabaret, which primary entailed dancing, and others combined dancing with occasional sex work. Maja, for example, left Russia and came to Ukraine where her mother lived. Once in Ukraine she left for Lebanon where she worked as a cabaret dancer on a three-month contract basis. Oksana and Ana both worked in a cabaret in Serbia where agents proposed that they switch to sex work in Italy. While Oksana relocated directly to Italy, Ana arrived a couple of months later having first returned home to Moldova. Others again alternated entertainment work with petty trade. Snezana undertook several trips from Moldova to Turkey in order to buy and sell goods at the market. During one of these trips she met a young Turkish man whom she subsequently married. After four years in Turkey, Snezana returned to Moldova and, approximately a year later, she left for Italy for entertainment work in a nightclub.

That women's migrating to Italy did not occur due to a third party's forceful intervention becomes discernible if attention is paid to the amount of time that passed between when women first contacted a third party and the actual moment of departure. When studies take this aspect of the migratory process into consideration, the results indicate a lapse of a week or less between initial contact with a third party and the actual departure. Scholars use this data as evidence of the organisational capabilities and swift functioning of 'trafficking' networks (Orfano, 2003: 199). My data present only one case that supports such a claim. In the case of Ivana, there was less than a week gap between when she was first approached by a third party and her decision to accept the offer. The third party imposed on Ivana a quick departure in order to manipulate the respondent easier and to keep up the deception about the type of the work she was expected to perform abroad. The specificity of Ivana's example is that it constitutes the only account that conforms to the trafficking definition in terms of transportation of persons by means of coercion or deception into slavery-like conditions. For all other women, the process of deciding whether or not to leave lasted considerably longer, at times lasting even between six months and a year.

To give an example, it took Liudmila six months to decide whether she wanted to do sex work as a condition for migrating to Italy. Sasha took approximately the same amount of time to decide about her departure. First, she contacted an agency arranging visas and work abroad. The agency offered her cabaret work in Japan. Shortly before departing for Japan, Sasha spoke with a group of women recently back from working in street prostitution in Italy. While what they told her made her doubt the validity of her decision to migrate, one of the women who just returned from Italy convinced Sasha that Italy was a good place to work. Sasha consequently decided to migrate to Italy for sex work, taking some additional time to arrange her first intercourse so as to know – as she put it – 'what these things are like'. For Ioanna, the process of deciding took about a year. Initially, when another respondent suggested they leave together to work in a cabaret in Serbia, she refused. A year later, the same friend asked her again whether she would consider leaving for Italy for street sex work. Ioanna decided to give it a go and during the months preceding the departure inquired what sex work consists of and how to do it and started learning Italian so as to be able to orientate herself better once in Italy.

These women's migration to Italy was not an abrupt act orchestrated by a third party. It rather evolved out of their social-economic context and their individual needs and desires. As respondents' migratory histories and the span of time that preceded their decision to migrate dispute the distinctiveness of 'trafficking' operations and signal a close similarity to other forms of labour migration, I turn to examine the interaction between women and third parties that resulted in their leaving for Italy.

Recruitment process or meeting the right people

In the studies on 'trafficking', the term recruitment is typically used to indicate a person who 'first proposed or imposed the travel abroad to the victim by means of fraudulent or open offer' (Orfano, 2003: 196). Scholars by now agree that the sensational narrative of women being kidnapped and forced into prostitution, still dear to the press, is more the exception than the rule (UNICEF et al., 2002: 7; Maluccelli, 2001). My study also presents such an exception. Only one respondent, Ivana, was deceived the about type of the work and coerced into migration to Italy through the use of force. A man and a woman approached Ivana while she worked in a neighbourhood bar in the suburbs of Zagreb, the capital of Croatia. The couple offered her a job as a waitress in Switzerland. Ivana and her husband met with the couple to arrange the travel details and agreed for the departure to take place the following day. On the day of departure, Ivana arrived at the couple's house and was told she would be going to Italy and not to Switzerland. They also told her that in Italy her job would be to collect money from other women working in street prostitution. When Ivana refused, the male trafficker punched her in the eye and threatened her with further violence. After being kept in a third party's apartment for some days while he was making the travel arrangements, Ivana was brought to Italy against her will. In this case, the respondent was approached directly by the recruiters, deceived about the type of work, coerced into leaving for Italy by the use of physical violence and finally worked under highly exploitative conditions in street prostitution for the same third party who recruited her in her country of origin.

While Ivana's account of her arrival in Italy corresponds to the UN Protocol's classification of what constitutes trafficking, other women's experiences do not fit the same pattern. Respondents' accounts of how they got in touch with third parties and who these were complicate the view that women's migration is the outcome of third parties' organised and intentional action. My data indicate that often the first contact with those who informed the respondents of the possibility to work abroad or proposed that they migrate for work (whether sex work or not) took place within the respondents' network of acquaintances, namely their female friends who had already migrated or were themselves acquainted with others who were working abroad. Women often initiated the first contact by asking their female acquaintances if they knew of people who could organise their trip and find work for them abroad. Following this initial exchange of information, respondents were usually referred to an individual or an agency that provided the services they were looking for.

An example of this pattern emerges from the accounts of Larisa and Liudmila from Moldova, both of whom wanted to reach Italy, where female friends of theirs worked in street prostitution. These friends, who had been living in Italy for several years already, promised to help the respondents in looking for a 'normal' job.[3] One of these friends sent Liudmila money in order to apply for a visa. However, at that moment Liudmila found no agency able to arrange an Italian visa. In order to solve the visa issue, the friend put the respondent in contact with a person who could help Liudmila reach Italy on condition that she worked in prostitution: 'She called me another time and told me: "I'll give you the phone number of a man who will help you to come to Italy. But, to work on the street", she said. So, later … I called, I left and I came here to Italy'. Similarly, Larisa's friend in Italy put her in contact with a man who agreed to take her to Italy. Without being charged any transportation fee, the respondent was promised that she would reach Italy in ten days. Prior to departure, Larisa was inserted in a group of four young women who were all about to leave for Italy, among them a friend of hers returning to Italy for the third time.

Contrary to the experiences of Liudmila and Larisa, Oksana was contacted by a 'recruiter' previously unknown to her and asked whether she would be interested in leaving Ukraine and going to work in a nightclub in Serbia. In my interview with her, Oksana described this encounter in terms of a proposition rather than an imposition from the side of the recruiter. The respondent's description of how, on several occasions, she was recruited for labour abroad, offers an example of the variety of actors involved in the 'recruitment' process. Her account also illustrates the ways in which a migrant woman who has acquired knowledge about labour migration passed that information on to others and proposed to others to enter a sex work contract too. During a ride home in a taxi, Oksana started a conversation with the driver about the difficult economic situation in Ukraine. Both she and the driver complained about the lack of work. After a while, the driver asked if Oksana knew of women who would be interested in working abroad in a nightclub in Serbia. They exchanged phone numbers in case the respondent came to think of anyone who might be interested in the offer. Some months later the taxi driver phoned the respondent to ask her again whether she knew of any women willing to leave and work abroad. Oksana recounts the event as follows:

[He:] 'So Oksana, are there any girls who want to go abroad?'
I say 'No, there are not.'
[He:] 'And you, what do you think? Did you find a job?'
I say 'No, nothing. Nothing changed. Everything has worsened.'
Then he told me: 'If you would like to leave'
[She:] 'I don't know. I have to think about it.'
[He:] 'For how long do you need to think?'
[She:] 'I don't know. About two weeks.'

When, some weeks later, the respondent decided to leave Ukraine together with a female friend for Serbia, she phoned the taxi driver who then put them in contact with a woman running an agency. The woman explained about the type of work in the nightclub, handled their travelling arrangements and accompanied Oksana, her friend and a couple of other women to Novi Sad in Northern Serbia. After two weeks of work in the nightclub, the third party who managed Oksana's work in the club suggested that she leave Serbia for sex work in Italy. The respondent agreed, left for Italy and, having fulfilled her three-month contract, returned to Ukraine. Some months later, a female friend with whom Oksana worked in prostitution phoned her from Italy and asked whether she would like to return to Bologna and work together again. While deciding if she should leave or not, Oksana asked another friend of hers, Ioanna, to join her. In order to buy the bus tickets, they borrowed the money from the Albanian boyfriend of the woman who originally invited Oksana to Bologna. After an agency arranged for the visas, Oksana and Ioanna purchased the tickets and left Ukraine for Italy. In Bologna, both women came to prostitute for the Albanian who lent them the money for the visa fee and the bus fare. Contrary to the newspaper clippings at the beginning of this chapter that describe them as unaware, deceived and 'illegal', Olga and Natasha, the pseudonyms for Oksana and Ioanna, carefully planned their migratory project, entered into a sex work contract with a third party and arrived in Italy with valid travel documents.

As these accounts illustrate, agencies play an important role in the migratory process. While some women contacted agencies in order to arrange their visa and/or travel to Italy, others turned to agencies to assist them in finding work. Contact with the agencies occurred by word of mouth or by direct contact: namely, women got in touch with an agency after reading an advertisement for work abroad in a local paper. The agencies are differently organised and vary in size and in the services offered. Some agencies specialise in facilitating travel, others in employment and some in both (Anderson and O'Connell Davidson, 2003; Pastore et al., 1999). As we can see from the following example, agencies arrange and profit from organising the movement of migrants or from acting as intermediaries between migrants and third parties recruiting women for sex work in Italy. Ana, who lived in Moldova, initially contacted an agency because she wanted to leave for Moscow and do sex work there. She was discouraged, however, by a female friend of hers who told her that in Moscow the police are likely to arrest her immediately upon arrival, and that going to Moscow in the middle of the Russian winter was a bad idea anyway. Lacking an alternative solution, the respondent settled for Moscow nevertheless and went to an agency to inquire again about her leaving:

> I went to see her [the woman working at the agency] and there was a person, a man, who brings girls to Italy. But back then I did not know it. I immediately asked her 'How is it going with my leaving for Moscow?' and she told me that a woman should be coming from Moscow to meet me and talk to me. I asked when and she told me that the woman did not arrive yet but that she should be here in two weeks. That man, as soon as he saw me, he told me: 'Why do you want to leave for Moscow? Why can't you go to Italy? You look good, very good'. You know, I glanced at him and I told him 'I have no documents' and he said 'That's no problem, I'll get them for you'. 'Then, OK', [I said]. You know, I felt happy. I went back to my friend and I told her all, because you know, he said he will take her too.

As in the case of Oksana and Iaonna, this episode also points to the difficulty in separating clearly between informal networks and formal agencies or (individual) private recruiters when investigating the way in which women arranged the travel logistics. At the same time as Ana negotiated her departure to Italy she also arranged for a female friend of hers to leave too. Ana relied on an informal network comprised of friends or acquaintances to gain initial information about migrating abroad rather than being approached by a person unknown to her who then coerced her into migrating. The majority of respondents did not portray their initial contact with individual recruiters or agencies as abusive. Rather, in Oksana's words, they are those who 'help girls to find a job in a foreign country'. Taxi drivers, restaurant owners and housewives all facilitated respondents' contacts with the agencies. These networks constituted the initial link in the 'chain of facilitation', which at later stages included a number of other actors such as sub-agents, document facilitators, employment agencies and/or travel agents (Anderson and Ruhs, 2008). All of these appear to be an integral part of the local and informal economies in respondents' countries of origin. Through such networks, a variety of individuals supplement their income through contacts and clients. As we will see in the next chapter, individuals and agencies on whose assistance women relied in order to reach Italy were not necessarily the ones who passed them the initial information, and were also not the same individuals who kept them in confinement and exploited their labour in street prostitution upon arriving in Italy. Informal networks, individual recruiters and agencies among others all intervene at different stages of the process, often having no interest in controlling and/or exploiting migrants' labour but instead profit from the recruitment and movement of persons. Similar profiles of small-scale informal networks have also been found to operate in cases of independent migrant sex workers, such as undocumented Latin American women working in indoor establishments in the Spanish-Portuguese frontier region (Ribeiro and Sacramento, 2005). These widely recurrent patterns of recruitment and travelling call into question the notion that an exploitative or abusive labour situation in the sex sector is the outcome of coerced migration or third parties' organised and intentional action to profit from migrant women's labour in prostitution.

Reconsidering deception

In order for the 'recruitment' process to be considered 'trafficking', the third party needs to carry out some kind of deceit with regard to the promises made to the migrants. In the debate surrounding 'trafficking' for the sex industry, a debate that has seen the direct involvement of large numbers of feminists, the discussion has evolved around the question whether women did or did not know that they will be working in prostitution. The available research has shown that a considerable percentage of migrant women agreed to work in the sex industry but were unaware of the living and working conditions in the countries of destination (Orfano, 2003; Gülçür and İlkkaracan, 2002; Maluccelli, 2001; McDonald et al., 2000). While this is an important aspect to highlight, in particular as situations of exploitation in the sex sector are often viewed as a consequence of deception about the nature of the work, it is also necessary to consider that when the emphasis is placed on deception (or lack of it), the analysis of 'trafficking' remains caught in the web of moral arguments surrounding prostitution. Unaccounted for remain the terms of agreement reached (or not) between the parties concerning specific living and working arrangements.

It is obvious that those women who were promised jobs as waitresses or domestic workers and were then inserted into the sex industry had not been informed about the terms of their sex-work contract. However, neither have they negotiated the terms of the contract for work in a restaurant or a private home. This situation is not much different to the one in which women agreed to sex work but knew very little about the concrete working conditions. As an illustration, we can look at the account of Kateryna. Having accepted her lover's offer to migrate from Romania to Italy and work as a prostitute, Kateryna was not aware of the conditions in which she would be working, such as the long hours, the high number of clients and the constant control by a third party or peers. Reflecting on her decision to go to Italy, Kateryna commented:

> He [the boyfriend] told me what my job would be and I thought that's fine since it won't be written on my forehead what I've done. I decided to go for a year because he promised me half of the amount I would make while working as a prostitute. I thought that after a year I'll have quite some money. Then I could return home, finish my studies and make something better out of my life. But the whole thing turned out more complicated than I thought.

Knowing little about the specificities of the setting of her new job, Kateryna agreed to a one-year contract and a 50-50 pay share.

The vagueness concerning the terms of work is typical also of the accounts of those respondents who said that they knew everything in advance about sex work. Oksana, who was about to return to Italy for the second time, described to her friend Ioanna her previous experience of street prostitution and asked her if she would consider coming along next time. Ioanna described arriving in Bologna for sex work with the following words: 'I came to Italy and I knew all about it – what to tell to the clients, what to do, where to go – I knew it all.' Yet a closer analysis of the respondent's narrative shows that by 'I knew it all' Ioanna meant that Oksana described how the monetary 'exchange' between a prostitute and client works. This was explained with an explicit conversation in which Ioanna was told that she would be working specifically in street prostitution. In this way, Oksana equipped Ioanna with information she herself did not have the first time she went to Italy for sex work. Oksana, as a number of other respondents who entered into the sex work contract with third parties thought that they would be working indoors (cabaret or nightclub) rather than on the street. So, even though Oksana shared with Ioanna her previous experience of street sex work and they negotiated the pay and the length of the stay, they expected to work independently and reimburse the third party the money he lent them to pay for the visa and travel fare. The respondents did not expect that they would have to surrender most of their earnings to the third party and prostitute under conditions of confinement that made it difficult to step out of the contract:

> We came here but we did not think that we would be working for someone. We thought that she [third party's girlfriend and a friend of Oksana] would look for a place [on the street] for us. [We thought that] she would find us a place. It is OK to work for a month for someone as to return the money he gave us. We would work in order to pay back the expenses, for the help he gave us in coming here. We thought that ... we would be on our own and ... not working for someone else who is always around.

The fact that women consented to sex work was no guarantee that upon their arrival in Italy they would have been able to work independently of the third party and keep their earnings; neither did it mean that they were in control of their working conditions and free of exploitation and abuse.

Contrary to what might be expected, for some respondents the terms of the contract did not play a key role in their migratory project. They were less interested in the earning potential of prostitution, but used the sex work contact instead as a means of reaching Italy. A quote from Ana's interview illustrates this situation best:

> He said his name was Renzo. He explained everything to me: how we are supposed to work, how much money we get – ten percent of all the money is for us – how we'll get in trouble if we make a mistake. See, he was trying to scare us. But me, you know, I was thinking 'Just get me to Italy'. To everything he would say I would reply 'Yes, yes, yes' and hoped he would choose me for Italy. Once in Italy, I'd have taken care of it all by myself.

While some degree of deception about the working conditions in sex work can be found in all respondents' accounts, a narrow focus on whether women consented or not to prostitution hinders a comprehensive analysis of labour arrangements in third party controlled street prostitution and in considering that some women might not be concerned about the working conditions at all, as they saw the contract with the third party merely as a means to an end. Anderson and O'Connell Davidson (2003) argue that the concept of deception as put forth by the definition of trafficking leaves open questions about the extent of deception needed in terms of job content, rates of pay, working practices, work rate and length of the contract among others in order to qualify as a VoT. If, according to the UN Protocol, a case of 'trafficking' takes place when, by means of deception, a person has been recruited and transported by a third party into exploitative working conditions so as to profit from her labour, then the ambiguity lies with the notion of deception itself. The fact that the definition of trafficking presupposes an interrelation between deception and subsequent exploitation of migrants on the part of 'traffickers' conflates the range of interests third parties might have in supplying vague information concerning the working contract. Third parties might profit from migrants' recruitment or travel rather than from their labour. The vagueness of the notion of deception, together with force, coercion and exploitation as distinctive components of trafficking then establish an oversimplified and ultimately erroneous demarcation between voluntary and involuntary processes of migration. This is particularly important since violence, coercion, deception and exploitation may also occur in voluntary and legally regulated systems of migration and employment.

The difference borders make

In tackling issues relative to women's travel and work arrangements, there is a need to ask specific and rather detailed questions about the travel itself. Some of the questions I ask in the following sections are: in what ways and with whom did women cross the border and reach their destination? Were they undocumented or did they possess passports and visas? If they were in possession of a visa, how did they obtain it and for how long were those visas valid? In posing these questions, this section aims to make visible the ways in which immigration and visa regulations and border controls contributed to creating conditions that exposed migrant women to heightened levels of vulnerability and labour exploitation.

Dealing with visa and border controls

Dependency on a third party or an agency to arrange travel to Italy is due to the tightening of formal EU migratory channels for certain groups of people. In fact, none of the women would have qualified for an

EU tourist visa which would have allowed them to enter at an official border post and travel with 'regular' means of transportation. Being granted a tourist visa requires a considerable number of documents that the respondents were not able to provide. These include: a passport, proof of the purpose of the visit namely an invitation letter (from an Italian citizen), a return ticket, confirmation of accommodation, evidence of sufficient funds, evidence of medical insurance and, in the case of work or study, also a letter from the employer or school certifying a labour contract or school enrolment. Most of the women could have fulfilled one, at most two, of the above requirements since none of them knew a person who could have acted as a guarantor for them or could provide evidence of sufficient funds to finance their stay in Italy. Moreover, a visa applicant is requested to present herself in person, which requires additional funding especially when the visa granting Consulate is not where woman lives but may be, at times, as far off as a neighbouring state. Not only is being granted a visa a long, troublesome and expensive process, as different NGO sources report, but Consulates also often make the process deliberately more difficult by establishing a number of rules and procedures that make it extremely difficult for certain groups of people to obtain visas (Apap, 2001).

An example of the difficulty to obtain official permission to enter Italy through a Consulate is illustrated by Svjeta's account. Svjeta was in possession of the residence and work permit granted in Italy specifically to VoTs under Article 18 of the Italian Immigration Law. She left Italy for a short visit to Ukraine in order to visit her daughter and husband with whom she had had little contact over the past few years. Shortly before returning to Italy, the husband confiscated her Italian residence permit so that she could not leave for Italy. Being unable to convince him to give her back the document, as at that time there was no visa-granting Italian consulate in Ukraine, Svjeta travelled to the Italian Consulate in Budapest, with the intention of obtaining a copy of the permit and returning to Italy. At the Consulate, she explained that she had lost her residence permit and asked the Consulate employees to assist her in returning to Italy. She was told that she could not return to Italy and her request for a visa was not granted. Following the rejection, Svjeta contacted the Women's Shelter in Bologna, which, according to Article 18, was respondent's legal guarantor and assisted her in fulfilling the obligations linked to the residence permit. The Women's Shelter intervened by calling the Consulate, an operation that took considerable time since it was extremely difficult to reach the person handling the respondent's case, and, upon the Consulate's request, sent a letter of guarantee for the respondent and a copy of respondent's residence permit. The Consulate replied that those documents were not sufficient to grant an entry visa for Italy. At this point the Women's Shelter asked the Head of the Foreigners' Police in Bologna to intervene, who then sent an additional letter of guarantee and confirmed the authenticity of the respondent's residence permit. Once more, the Consulate replied that these documents were insufficient, and requested that the Head of the Foreigners' Police call in person, only then granting the respondent an entry visa.

As well as illustrating the difficulties migrant women might encounter when attempting to obtain a visa on their own, this episode points to the costs involved in such an operation. The respondent had to cover her travel expenses from Ukraine to Hungary as well as the costs of several hotel stays. Since the whole procedure took more then four weeks, Svjeta considerably overstayed the time she had taken off from her job and was consequently fired. Even though a third party might charge more than the official Consulate's visa rates,[4] women know that they are not likely to obtain a visa without contacts and a large sum of money. Yet in certain situations even agencies who specialised in visa procedures found it impossible to arrange a visa. A striking example comes from Liudmila, who hired an agency to arrange her visa and organise the travel to Italy. Yet due to the instability in the region caused by NATO's bombing of Serbia, the agency in Moldova was not able to carry out this otherwise routine operation.[5] After months of waiting for the situation to change, Liudmila finally decided to contact a third party, who arranged for undocumented travel and brought the respondent to Italy in four days under the condition that she work in prostitution.

Respondents' accounts point to women's awareness of needing to cross the borders secretly. Kateryna puts it like this: 'Some girls travel hidden in the back of a truck. They take sleeping pills in order not to do anything and not to eat at all. They take sleeping pills and sleep during the entire journey'. She herself was unsuccessful in crossing the border into Austria:

> It was 11 pm when they left me in the forest. It was really dark – it was September – it was a crazy darkness and it started to rain. I walked by my guide, the one who knew the path, but forgot it. I walked from 11 pm until 8 in the morning and it was a nightmare. When I think back on it, I don't know how I did it. I was tired, and I was covered in mud because I fell down. It is like walking on the ground you do not know, where it is dark, rainy, there are holes filled with mud that you do not see. I fell many times, I was totally dirty, covered

in mud, it was humid and I said 'I am giving up'. I was so tired that I was walking on all fours. I could not stand straight any longer. It was three girls with the guide. I said 'I have to do it, I have to, I have to.' I always thought that I had to do it, that I have to reach the destination; I could not stay here in the middle of the forest. I don't know, at one point, at 8 am, it was becoming light; we were not reaching the point where the car was waiting for us. I could not walk any longer and the guide said 'I'm going and if the car is there, I'll come back to pick you up.' He left and I fell asleep on the ground. After the night of walking, I could not keep my eyes open any longer. And the other girls were pulling me 'No, you cannot sleep here, wake up otherwise you will get a lung infection' and they forced me to get up. The muscles on my legs were not holding me anymore. He was not coming back and we couldn't stay there, we were hungry and thirsty. When we came out of the forest, we started walking the same road he did. Slowly, slowly and we'll get there [we thought]. At 8 am we passed by a small village, there must have been only 4 houses there, and someone who got up early saw us from the window and called the police. They got me.

For Kateryna, the unsuccessful crossing resulted in deportation from Austria. For Larisa, also apprehended by the border police, the arrest meant prohibition of entry into Hungary. A few weeks later, each of the respondents embarked upon another crossing via a different route. Larisa arrived in Italy from Albania by boat, while Kateryna crossed the Slovenian-Italian border on foot. Kateryna comments on her second journey: 'I was scared of being caught and sent back home. Because if they [the border police] would have caught me, I would have had to do it all over again'. The above quotation underlines the determination and the wilful intent of the women to succeed in crossing the border, which challenges descriptions of coerced and involuntary migration put forward by the notion of 'trafficking'.

Not all respondents arrived in Italy undocumented; agents provided some women with the necessary travel documents. Realising that she would have to cross the border on foot because the third party was initially not willing to spend money to buy her a visa, Snezana refused to leave until she successfully negotiated a visa and a bus ride to Italy. Another respondent, Tatiana, flew from Moscow to Rome with a 15-day tourist visa arranged for her by two Russian women working as prostitutes in Italy. Oskana and Ionna, alias Olga and Natasha from the newspaper clipping mentioned in the introduction to this chapter, reached Italy in two days having travelled by bus. Contrary to what the paper reports, they did not enter Italy undocumented but with short-terms visas arranged through an agency with money borrowed from a third party. This money covered the costs of the visa, travel from Ukraine to Poland, a night in a hotel in Warsaw and a bus ticket to Bologna.

Women's accounts suggest first, then, that not all migrants who are irregular have entered into the EU via irregular channels. The women who travelled with a visa became undocumented after having over-stayed the length of the granted visa. These considerations need to be read in the light of EU governments' position that trafficking equals illegal migration that must be deterred via stricter border policing. The existing research for Italy offers a different picture of migratory flows. First, the data by the Italian Ministry of Internal Affairs indicate that the majority of third-country nationals residing illegally in the country have not crossed its borders undocumented but have entered the country with valid entry clearance, becoming undocumented either once their visas expired or after they overstayed their residence permits (Caritas/Migrantes, 2005). Second, it is extremely problematic to endorse a model that positions trafficking as a form of illegal migration in opposi-tion to legally approved modes of migration. Trafficking may have legal elements such as legally obtained visas. Conversely, legal migratory processes may involve illegal components such as requests for high fees advanced by the agencies or even illegal payments asked by Consulates. If arranging a visa is not cheap and easy, migrants will not be able to access, even when available, formal governmental migratory channels (Anderson and O'Connell Davidson, 2003). Instead, they will resort to irregular channels that, as I discuss in the following section, in turn take advantage of migrants' legal vulnerability whether by charging higher costs for travel and documents or by profiting from their labour.

Risk of violence and vulnerability during undocumented migration

Having or not having a visa is linked to the ways in which the women crossed the borders and to the duration of time required for the crossing. The difference between documented and undocumented border crossings is most apparent in the narratives of those respondents who travelled to Italy twice: first time on foot without a visa and a second time by bus with a tourist visa. When women crossed the bor-ders undocumented on foot, in a truck or by boat, descriptions of the journey constituted a central element of their migration narrative and included detailed descriptions of the events and actors involved. For example, Oksana recalled the number and names of other travellers, the weather conditions when they crossed the Slovenian-Italian border, the vegetation and even the conditions of the ground they walked on. When respondents returned to Italy for the second time with a valid visa and travelled by plane or bus they crossed the borders quickly and smoothly. In stark contrast to the narratives of their first border crossing, in their accounts of the 'legal' crossing women remember very few details about the journey. We can attribute the disparity between descriptions of undocumented and documented forms of travel to the degree of danger or risk the respondents underwent during the 'illegal' experience. The fear of being caught by the border police, being sexually abused, contracting a disease during the prolonged travel, or having little or no control over the terms of the travel and therefore being dependent on the third party, all produce a highly traumatic experience that women remember in quite some detail.

The longer the journey became, the more the respondents were exposed to the risk of abuse or sexual violence from agents, contracting a disease or developing a dependency on alcohol to deal with the conditions of travel. Moreover, arranging for transportation without any initial capital to pay for the cost of the travel meant incurring a debt with the agents. As the journeys got longer, the amount of debt increased and respondents became increasingly vulnerable to violence and labour exploitation during the journey. Larisa's story exemplifies well the vulnerability induced by debt-migration. After being deported from Hungary, Larisa contacted another agent in Moldova who promised her that she would reach Italy in ten days; Larisa set off for a journey that lasted two months and that took her across the Balkans. Reconstructing the respondent's travel route, it emerges that each undocumented border crossing had a monetary value. Larisa contracted a debt at each border because she could not cross at official border posts as she was not in possession of a visa. To pay back these debts, Larisa took short-term jobs working in cabarets at different points in the journey. Starting her travel in Moldova and needing no visa to enter Romania, Larisa first crossed the Moldovan-Romanian border without being exposed to any type of abuse.[6] At the border between Romania and Serbia, the group with which the respondent travelled stopped at the banks of the river Danube. Being transported to the other side of the river and thus crossing into Serbia entailed being passed against payment from one agent to the other, and being able to continue the journey only once the transaction had taken place: 'People would come with a ferry, they would look at us and if they would like us, they would take us. ... They would pay money and you went'. The consequence of this transaction was that the respondent contracted a debt towards the third party who paid money for her and that that person acquired power over her by means of this monetary transaction. Larisa comments on this power disparity with the following words: 'One feels like a dog. You cannot say anything because he paid money for you. There's nothing to be done. It's ugly.'

In order to pay off the debt of 750 EUR so she could continue to travel to Italy, the respondent had to work in a cabaret in Serbia in a situation where she had no control over her earnings. This situation considerably reduced Larisa chances to negotiate the amount of time to be spent in the cabaret and the amount of money to be paid 'back'. Continuing her travels towards Italy via Albania meant undergoing a similar process once again. The continuation of travel was now in the hands of a 21-year-old Albanian man who abused Larisa sexually by imposing unprotected intercourse on her. In order to go through this period, Larisa made heavy use of liquor and was in a permanent state of drunken stupor. When confiding her desperation to a female friend of hers with whom she travelled, the friend told her to persevere because she overheard that their travel to Italy was to be organised within a week. Shortly afterwards the respondent undertook a one-week boat journey that took her from Albania to Italy where she was met by the very same third party who had abused her in Albania. Based on the debt Larisa contracted in order to reach Italy, the Albanian man continued to exercise power over the respondent by controlling and profiting from her labour in street prostitution. The respondent's undocumented status resulted in her contracting debt and making her dependent on third parties in order to continue her travel. This situation increased Larisa's vulnerability to violence and exploitation and allowed third parties to gain control and achieve profit from exploiting her labour.

In addition to being vulnerable to abuse by third parties, undocumented status exposes migrants to ill-treatment that often accompanies undocumented migrants' apprehensions by border police. An example comes from Kateryna who got intercepted by the border police when crossing undocumented into Austria:

> We were undergoing an interrogation: 'What car brought you here? What was your destination? Who are you? Who brought you here?' We would give the first information that crossed our mind and they would see that we are making it up. I was tired; my eyes were closing constantly. I am a smoker and I ran out of cigarettes. The inspector looked at me and she asked me: 'Do you smoke?' I said yes, and she asked me if I would like a cigarette. When I answered yes,

she said: 'Then, what is the colour of the car that brought you here?' After the whole day of interrogation, the police brought us to a cell at midnight and they even handcuffed my friend.

Following the arrest, the respondent was detained in prison for three weeks until the unit that arrested her obtained funds from the government to cover the costs of her deportation to Romania, namely the costs of the train ticket to the Hungarian-Romanian border. The train ticket for the remaining 300 kilometres that separated the respondent from her town of residence was paid with the money given to the respondent as a present by a Pakistani male migrant detained in the same prison. Having being deported meant that Kateryna was barred from utilising formal migration channels in the future, which in her case meant she would not have been able to obtain an EU visa for the next five years. Deportation then increased the respondent's dependency on individual recruiters or agencies to reach Italy and exposed her to additional risk of abuse that migrants encounter during undocumented travel.

My data show that in their aim to channel migrants into legally sanctioned migration schemes and prevent labour exploitation in countries of destination, visa regulation and border controls produce situations that, in fact, increase migrants' vulnerability to abuse and exploitation, and the involvement of third parties in facilitating travel and employment arrangements. Consideration of the link between border controls and conditions of vulnerability need, therefore, to be taken into account by scholars of trafficking because the border is a significant element of anti-trafficking policies (Segrave, 2009) and laws regulating the conditions of entry into the EU contribute to rendering migrant women vulnerable to abuse and labour exploitation during their travel and, as I discuss in Chapter 3, at their destination. Hence, far from preventing trafficking, stricter immigration controls have unintentional consequences, such as serving the economic interests of third parties by increasing the amount of migrants' debt and raising the level of control these third parties exercise over migrants. Quite paradoxically, immigration regulations that aim at suppressing 'trafficking' and hampering the illegal movements of people work in favour of third parties as these become an alternative to the formally sanctioned EU migratory channels.

Projects of autonomy

In her analysis of how 'sex trafficking' is constructed and operates as a discourse, Jo Doezema suggested that the recurrent incidence of the term 'poverty' in relation to 'sex trafficking' functions as a rhetorical device that locates migrant women in prostitution as innocent victims and secures the victim/villain binary (Doezema, 1999). In accordance to Doezema's suggestion, migrant women from eastern Europe working in the sex industry in the EU, are commonly portrayed as victims of deceit or coercion, or as victims of pressing poverty, which is given as the reason why they left their home countries. This emphasis on poverty leads to a rather problematic reading of migration in terms of a rational economic action. Understanding poverty merely in terms of economic deprivation, as I show in the following sections, fails to consider the role poverty plays in relation to women's subjectivities and obscures a plethora of factors and desires that inform women's migratory projects.

Poverty

When asked what brought them to Italy, the motivation women most frequently put forth is that of poverty. Reference to poverty and economic hardship typically opened most of the respondents' accounts. Poverty, as in case of Ioanna, is used to describe a situation in which the income of the family barely sufficed to cover basic needs such as food and housing: 'You know, back home we are not that well off. Back home my mum and I worked at the market but the money we would earn was hardly enough to buy food'. Poverty is also used to describe the difficult living conditions of not having running water in the house or, in Kateryna's story, always having to go to school in the same pair of torn shoes. The description of economic hardship is also used to refer to the situation of not being compensated for the work done. To give an example, Ana recounted how while working in a meat factory she did not get any wage but instead received some meat to take home. This situation went on for a couple of months until the factory went bankrupt and all the workers lost their jobs.

It is unquestionable that the lives of women and their families have been affected by economic hardship. In the literature, poverty is considered for the consequences it has on women's and girls' employment and education and is often quoted as a trigger to women's migration. While regional differences should be taken into account when considering the impact of economic restructuring on women's lives, as a general trend scholars agree that women's socio-economic situation has worsened across eastern Europe and that economic restructuring has affected women more severely than men (Becker-Schmidt, 2002: 8). Economic restructuring entailed a transition from a planned to a market economy and the subsequent liberalisation of trade that overlapped with the process of European integration. The pressure to be competitive resulted in the reduction of spending on welfare, food and agriculture subsidies as well as in cuts in healthcare and education (Adam, 2002: 12). The primacy the EU gives to its economic agenda and to a reconciliation of family and work in its gender-related policies in eastern Europe led to the deterioration of social and economic benefits for specific segments of population such as young women (Koncz, 2002; Siemeienska, 2002; Regulska, 2001; Roman, 2001). The cuts in public education resulted in the reduction of educational benefits, which had negative repercussions for women and girls.

The research project on women in transition economies completed by the International Helsinki Federation for Human Rights examined the status of women in 29 countries in eastern Europe and the former Soviet Union (fSU). The report signalled that, due to a high level of economic crisis and increased poverty, women present a high level of dropouts from school, especially in fSU, where the state abandoned control over compulsory education. In Moldova, girls' education has been affected at both primary and university levels, and the number of female students has greatly decreased. In Romania, for example, the difficulties created in the transition process resulted in high dropout rates in secondary schools. In Serbia, women have been moving out of education and into the 'informal' economy (IHF, 2000). When it comes to the labour issues, the report highlights increased levels of women's poverty and unemployment. For example, since 1997 in Romania, while both women and men are affected by high levels of unemployment (18–20 per cent), women are more exposed to unemployment due to their labour positions in sectors subject to economic restructuring (IHF, 2000: 350). In Moldova, where 80 per cent of the population lives in poverty, the economic crisis caused by restructuring and privatisation disproportionately affected women, and unemployment increased due to a reduction of personnel in low-income light industries employing mostly women (80–85 per cent). In comparison to 1994, when the rate of women's unemployment was 8.9 per cent, at the end of the 1990s the rate had increased to 17.8 per cent for women and 10.2 per cent for men (IHF, 2000: 314). In Ukraine a high level of underemployment is typical for women's labour. Women are highly educated but the level of education rarely corresponds to employment requirements. Due to the socio-economic crisis, women's employment rate has been declining since 1995, and some 3 million people lost jobs in 1997–8 due to the closing of production lines and received no wages. Consequently, one-third of the population profits from unofficial work and so-called shadow economies. Women form the majority of the population forced onto the streets and into selling and buying goods in the marketplace. Young women under the age of 30 are the most vulnerable in this situation and they amount to 44.3 per cent of the total number of unemployed women in Ukraine (IHF, 2000: 476).

Looking at education and labour is crucial in order to comprehend women's lives within the context of socio-economic restructuring. The respondents, aged between 20 and 30, belong to the first generation of young women who have been raised and educated in eastern European and fSU countries during the 'transition' period from socialism/communism to a neoliberal market economy. Poverty certainly played an important role in the development of women's desire to leave. However, the recurrence of the poverty theme put forward in women's narratives as the main reason for migrating is too significant to overlook. While the situation of economic necessity was a concrete fact that impacted the lives of women prior to migration and needs to be acknowledged as such, I suggest that, due to its recurrent position at the very opening of the narratives, the topic of poverty is best referred to as an isotropy that plays a crucial role in the construction of respondents' subjectivities. The scrutiny of the isotropy of poverty in relation to the life stories at large elicits a correlation between the theme of poverty and that of prostitution.

As I discuss in greater detail in Chapter 4, the motif of poverty operates as a mechanism through which women disavowed sex-work. In establishing an objective situation of poverty as the main factor behind their migration, women distanced themselves from the doubts that their working in prostitution is driven by sexual pleasure or financial greed. The emphasis on poverty at the very start of women's narratives sets up a discursive frame centred on economic need. Once this is established, women can return to it at different points of their narratives and reassert that they are not really prostitutes. For example, the respondents distinguished between the desire to possess money – characteristic of prostitutes – and the need to earn money, namely the circumstance they relate to their own experience of migration. They were also always careful to emphasise that they did not intend to keep the money for themselves but that they were doing it for someone else, such as their parents, sisters or children. Throughout the narratives, then, poverty reaffirms time and time again that the respondent is not a prostitute. Hence, I suggest, the reference to poverty needs to be examined beyond its immediate relation to economic need and in relation to its function in resisting the 'whore stigma' (Pheterson, 1996).

The prominence of the motif of poverty is also likely to conceal the fact that women's migratory projects developed out of a more complex set of factors and desires such as a pursuit of financial independence, an 'escape route' from patriarchal social relations (Anthias and Lazaridis, 2000: 7), a search for (emotional) autonomy from the family and ultimately a desire for mobility.

Lack of employment opportunities and the search for economic improvement

Prior to their departure for Italy, a number of respondents attended high school or university, some had a job and some worked and studied at the same time. Only a few of them had just primary school education while the majority completed secondary school, some type of professional school (e.g. medical nurses) or attended university. This concurs with results from other studies that point to the relatively high level of education of eastern European women in the sex industry. It also points to the fact that, before migrating, women were not unemployed but usually held a job in a variety of occupations such as factory work, petty trade, office work, nursing or teaching (Della Giusta et al., 2008: 65; Hopkins and Nijboer, 2004; Orfano, 2003). Being without work therefore was not, per se, a motivation for migrating. Rather, the impossibility of making ends meet even with a job and the lack of future prospects were factors that informed women's migratory projects. Respondents quite often spoke about the lack of prospects in words similar to Maja, who said: 'Looking for jobs at home was useless'. Alternatively, like Ana, they spoke in a disillusioned tone about the difficulty of achieving things in Moldova: 'In our country one doesn't manage to do things. One never finds money to do anything. One doesn't manage to do anything at all'. Sasha, who at the time was studying at the university in the capital of Ukraine, puts it in terms of the desire to change her financial situation: 'I have wanted to find some kind of work, some money for a long time. I couldn't stay there any longer: there was no money, no work, and I wanted to conclude my studies too'.

The lack of employment opportunities and future prospects provoked in women feelings of frustration and anger. Oksana described this situation as follows: 'Before coming to Italy I was always filled with anger. I was so nervous! Always ... [I asked myself] why was I born, where'll I find work, how'll we survive, how'll we get by?' The feeling of frustration was also due to pressure put on the respondent by other family members to look for employment. Oksana, who at the time was living with her mother, referred to it in this way: 'Back home there was a situation of crisis.

I needed to pay for the electricity, the phone ... I was always nervous, like a beast. I did not know what to do, where to go. Additionally, my aunt – the sister of my mother – would stop by and she kept telling me "You are not working! You are doing nothing!"' A number of other respondents did not frame the need for employment in terms of social expectations but, rather, stressed their awareness of the difficult economic situation of their families coupled with an understanding of the need to earn money and be economically self-sufficient. Ana, who had been a guest at her grand-mother's house after the fight with her mother, spoke of this awareness: '[In my grandmother's household] everyone has children, everyone has lit-tle money, they do not work, those who work, earn nothing. I am a grown up person, I cannot allow myself [to be maintained by them]. I myself do not approve of it either. It is better for me if I leave'. Ioanna speaks of that desire to leave and of the willingness to take the risk in realising it: 'I thought, "I'm leaving no matter what might happen. There's nothing to do here!"' As we can see, pressing poverty does not come up in women's narratives as a key determinant to migration. Rather, the accounts suggest that the lack of employment opportunities and/or future prospects, the desire for economic improvement and independence from the family, and a search for alternative resources all feature prominently in women's migration projects (Corso and Trifiro', 2003: 28).

Intra-family violence

Respondents' decisions to migrate were at times also influenced by fac-tors such as intra-family violence including physical and sexual abuse. While some women complained about sexual harassment at the work-place, a significant number of respondents were exposed to intra-family violence that most often took the form of physical abuse and, in one occasion, that of (attempted) incest. In Kateryna's case family violence was frequent. Her mother divorced the abusive father when Kateryna was six years old and remarried another violent man who, like the moth-er's previous husband, also sexually harassed the respondent. Another respondent, Ester, was caught in a family situation of physical violence and abuse: the father physically abused the mother and occasionally beat up the respondent as well. The father made all of the major decisions about the household and disobeying him would result in a beating. The violence reached its peak when, trying to impose absolute obedience, the father threatened the mother and two sisters with a firearm. While Ester identified strongly with her mother, she was also frustrated by her mother's lack of initiative and inability to leave the husband. In an emo-tionally loaded description of her parents, Ester told of how back then she had hated them both and expressed her need to separate herself from the mother: 'I think of my mother who is alone now [after the father has died], but there are also some neighbours and other people to keep her company. I had to leave sooner or later to live a life of my own. I could not always stay with her. There have been periods when I ran away [because] I wanted to leave the house'.

While mentioning episodes of violence here and there, the respondents always quickly glossed over them and never connected them explicitly – as they did in the case of poverty – to their migratory projects. Or, as in Ester's account of violence above, the respondents were more likely to speak of how the father was abusing the mother than of the abuse they themselves had experienced. This absence was due not only to the difficulty of talking about acts of abuse, or an indifference towards abuse that was perhaps considered common or ordinary and therefore a side issue, but also to the fact that bringing up the family abuse would have disrupted respondents' narrative of themselves as active agents. Intra-family violence has been found to constitute one of the factors that plays an important role in women's decision to migrate (Kofman et al., 2000). By not linking the violence suffered explicitly to the desire to leave, respondents distanced themselves from the position of a 'victim' and positioned themselves as protagonists of their migratory projects. As for other types of women's migration, the respondents stressed their determination to undertake a solo migration project and to support their families financially.

Projects of autonomy from the family

Disappointment and disagreement with parents, lack of respect, humiliation or a feeling of not being wanted all contributed to women's wishes for separation from the family, a desire for autonomy and the search for ways of realising it. An illustration comes from the account of Ivana who accepted the offer to work abroad hoping to earn enough money to support her husband and two children. That money would allow them to move out of her husband's parents' flat where they had no space of their own and were at the mercy of his parents' moods. There, they were constantly belittled: she for not being a good mother and he for not having a steady job. Ivana interpreted this unfriendliness as a sign of both families' disapproval of their marriage due to the fact that she comes from a Catholic Croatian family and her husband from a Muslim Bosnian background. Ivana and her husband looked at her short-term labour migration abroad as a way of improving their financial situation that would have allowed them to rent a flat on their own and live a more independent and less humiliating life.

Other respondents expressed a similar desire for autonomy from the family, usually communicated through episodes of disappointment towards one or both of their parents. Often they would portray their father as a drunkard or as an absent and abusive figure. Oksana was deeply disappointed that her father was drinking and unable to provide financially for her or the family. Snezana spoke of how she and her four siblings were abandoned by the mother who left when she could not any longer stand her husband's abuse. Snezana describes her own relationship with her father as nothing but a series of abuses of various kinds. Another respondent, Kateryna, had no relationship with her father and was disappointed with him because of his being a drunk. Yet, while avoiding him, she also wished for a caring relationship with her father. Her need of being taken care of was not compensated by her mother, who did not give her much attention or time:

> She married and remarried, and took me with her but I was there like a baggage would be. She never came to school, she never asked if I had eaten or not, never ever. Even when I went to the high school all the kids would come with their mothers who would ask the secretary how to do things. … [S]he was not interested in my life, what I was or was not doing. If I was absent for two days my mother would not even notice my absence. This was not because she did not love me but because she was like that.

In the same way that Kateryna perceives herself as a burden to her mother, so does another respondent, Ana. Ana's parents accused her of stealing money from them and threw her out of the house. She spent some time with her grandmother and then returned home. Ana describes with the following words the event that occurred upon her return home:

> I came back home and I thought that maybe they have realised what they did to me. Then mother and father told me 'Why did you come back? Why did you not stay where you were?' You know, when it is winter and you don't have a dress except the one you are wearing … I also had a bladder infection back then, I was bleeding. When they told me those things, I felt a pain in my heart. My grandmother is the person I loved most in my life and I know that she loves me too. But do you know what is the ugliest thing? I understood that they didn't need me. The mother, do you believe me, told me straight in my face, told me this 'I do not care for you. You earn your money where you want and the way you want!'

Recounted by means of direct speech and comparison, this episode is invested with the meaning of a breaking point from the family. A *staccato* effect, achieved using the direct speech to relay her mother's words, works to stress the veracity of mother's words. The comparison on the other hand contrasts the love of the mother to that of the grandmother allowing the respondent to conclude that the grandmother is the only one who ever truly loved her. Finally, relating sickness, blood and hurt to pain caused by the refusal of her parents works to identify her parents' rejection as a painful wound.

Hence, women's migratory projects also need to be read in relation to the desire to transform family relations rather than simply in terms of a pursuit of economic improvement to which references to poverty or economic hardship often reduce the impetus for migrating. For these young women, migration offered the opportunity to exit situations of family indifference or conflict and work towards achieving autonomy from the family. Respondents' willingness to take the risk and migrate needs then to be seen in terms of the desire to transform affective familiar ties and gain their parents' recognition and respect.

Ruptures and the search for alternative life projects

Relationship or marriage break-ups and a desire for a new male partner played a role in respondents' migratory projects too. While a number of respondents were at some point engaged or married, none of these arrangements was still in place at the time they departed for Italy.[7] Several respondents got married at the age of 18 and then divorced a year or two later. Oksana, on the other hand, got engaged and expected to marry not long before leaving for Italy. Yet the marriage was suddenly cancelled and her fiancé married another woman. Oksana saw a direct connection between the break-up and her leaving Ukraine for sex work:

> Six months after my boyfriend left me ... but me ... you know what I think? For example ... yes ... before I was always angry, I started really to hate him ... it is his fault that ... if he wouldn't have left me I could've been his wife. I could've been together with him; I could've not left to work on the street.

Oksana suggests that the break-up and being without a man affected her decision to leave for work in a nightclub in Yugoslavia first and for sex work in Italy later. This also seems to be confirmed by the fact that once the respondent returned from her first trip to Italy, she stayed for a while in Ukraine and then, unsuccessful in her attempt to find a husband, she left again. For those respondents who were divorced, as for example Liudmila and Marisa, the desire to find a partner also played an important role in their migratory projects. Liudmila told of a female friend of hers who left for Italy and found a man with whom she was happy and spoke of her own desire to meet someone: 'I also wanted to meet the right person; the right person to be together with'.

As well as affective ruptures, interrupted education influenced respondents' migratory projects. Sasha, who was studying economics, studied and worked at the same time. At a certain point she was no longer able to find a job and faced a financially difficult situation. She realised that if she was to find a job as an economist and make a career, she needed to learn English. Similarly, Liudmila began her university studies but, at one point, her family's financial situation worsened and they could not finance her education any more. As the 25 USD they earned per month in Ukraine and Moldova respectively was insufficient to cover their living and studying costs, both of the respondents opted for labour migration abroad as a way of earning money with the idea of continuing their university studies.

A very powerful effect on respondents was exercised by the situation that combined affective ruptures with that of interrupted education. Kateryna, who had virtually no relationship with her mother or father, saw in her secondary school teacher a key figure of reference and support. The respondent was one of the most brilliant students in the school and won the Romanian national school chemistry contest. When, due to problems in her family, Kateryna could no longer concentrate on studying and she repeatedly entered into conflict with other students and teachers, she lost the support of her favourite teacher. After her grades dropped drastically from excellent to poor, she decided to interrupt her education. Her self-esteem vanished and she sank into apathy:

> I was really stuck in Romania. Mentally I felt like being in a hole from which I couldn't come out any more. Because if you think of another girl with the same problems as I had, she could've made it even there but me, I was feeling down, no, I did not want anything any longer, I was depressed, depressed, depressed, and all the things I'd see – even school and friends – made me feel more down, and I didn't want to see them any more at all. And I was thinking only of running away; I was dreaming of running away. I didn't know precisely if I wanted to leave but I said to myself 'This life cannot continue like this, one cannot live like this.' Slowly the depression inside me was growing and I said 'A moment will arrive when I'll give up.'

Consequently, for Kateryna, migration became a way of breaking away from the desperate situation into which she had sunk. She departed from Romania wanting to break away from humiliation at school and violence at home: 'I wanted to start my life all over again in a place where no one knew me or things about me. I wanted to create a new image of myself'. Another respondent, Larisa, echoed this statement when she spoke of her leaving Moldova in terms of a hope for a different future: 'I ... came to Italy in order to change my life. A woman needs to take her life into her own hands, otherwise if she waits for things to change she ends up being 50 years old, achieving nothing and being no one, a zero.'

For these young women, then, migration emerges as a project offering an exit from situations characterised by lack of employment, loss of self-esteem, family abuse, interrupted education and a general sense of life stagnation.[8] For that reason, migration to Italy is prompted by women's desire to (re)conquer financial and affective mobility. To dilute the complexity of women's desires and projects to the narrative of victims would mean glossing over women's struggles against the structural inequalities that shape their lives and failing to understand third party-facilitated migration as an alternative migratory system for those who have no access to formal migratory channels.

Conclusion

Measures to counter 'trafficking' in women for the sex sector have been driven by the assumption that 'trafficking' is orchestrated by organised criminal networks and 'evildoers' who manipulate women into migrating and mislead them into sex work. The implication is that, when facilitated by third parties, women's migration for sex work gets construed as non-consensual and illegal and women primarily in terms of victims. This perspective leads to policy measures geared towards deterring 'trafficking' via strengthening of international cooperation between law enforcement agencies and tightening control over cross-border movements. Yet these legal interventions heighten, as Nicholas de Genova puts it, the visibility of 'illegal immigrants' and the invisibility of the law (De Genova, 2002). The emphasis on illegality locates the responsibility for the persistence of 'trafficking' with actors outside the EU and positions EU governments as being not implicated in the proliferation of irregular migration or situations of migrants' labour exploitation and vulnerability. Next to the observation that not all third party-facilitated migration is clandestine, this perspective fails to acknowledge that migrants are moving via irregular channels precisely due to the restrictions and controls imposed through EU legal interventions (Kapur, 2005). Stricter border controls and more restrictive immigration regulations do not protect migrants from abuse but rather make them dependent upon third parties to facilitate their migration and travel across international borders. Restrictive immigration regulations that aim to suppress 'trafficking' in fact criminalise the mobility of certain groups of people and paradoxically leave ample space for profiteering and the abuse of migrants. There is, therefore, a need to examine in greater detail the link between EU immigration regimes and migrant women's vulnerability to abuse and exploitation.

When the focus is on deterring irregular migration or combating the prevalence of organised crime, the perspective of the migrant subject is overlooked. And yet, when not identified a priori with victims, migrant women's perspectives disclose a complexity of cross-border movements that cannot be adequately addressed through binaries such as illegal versus legal and involuntary versus voluntary migration. Quite the contrary, migrant women's accounts of how they came to migrate disclose a complexity of desires and projects and such a level of determination to pursue those desires that to consign migrant women to the position of victims amounts to an act of epistemic violence. This is even more so as women's accounts of why and how they migrated are not exceptional, in the sense that they resemble other forms of women's transnational migration that see women as primary migrants. It is only by taking issue with the notions of coercion and deception and acknowledging migrant women's desire and pursuit of mobility that we can begin to address the uneasy question of how trafficking rhetoric and anti-trafficking legal interventions legitimate and contribute to setting up of hierarchies in labour and citizenship in the EU.

3
The Sex Trade

Entries: Conditions of confinement

'There is no freedom: you are in Italy but at the same time you are not. What does one see? Only the street and nothing else.'

Marisa

Introduction

Having arrived in Italy, all respondents worked in third party controlled street prostitution. In Chapter 2, I examined the so-called first phase of the 'trafficking' process and challenged the misconceptions of coercion and deception to show these women's desire to migrate and achieve mobility as well as their determination in pursuing these projects. In this chapter, I investigate what we can call the second phase of 'trafficking', namely the conditions of sexual exploitation, forced labour and slavery. For the sex sector, 'trafficking' is regularly referred to in terms of slavery with involuntariness and violence posited as its distinguishing features. The association between coercion and 'trafficking' might appear an obvious one. However, in order to understand the impact that the term coercion has in relation to 'trafficking', it is necessary to put it in the context of feminist contentions over prostitution. The process of negotiating the UN Trafficking Protocol was, in the words of Anne Gallagher, the Advisor on Trafficking to the UN High Commissioner for Human Rights, 'an unusual affair'. If the crime prevention system of the UN is usually of no interest to the international non-governmental community, on this occasion the Commission on Crime Prevention and Criminal Justice had to deal with unprecedented levels of NGO interventions (Gallagher, 2001: 1001). The bulk of these were advanced by feminist NGOs and the interventions concentrated on the issue of prostitution. There were two main coalitions to the contention. The first, the Human Rights Caucus,[1] stood by the position that prostitution is a form of legitimate labour, and the second, the International Human Rights Network,[2] was adamant that prostitution be seen as a violation of women's human rights.

Activists within the Human Rights Caucus argued that trafficking should be detached from its exclusive link to prostitution and viewed instead within the larger framework of labour rights abuses. They maintained that, along with work in the agriculture or garment industry, sex work is a form of globalised low-wage labour and insisted that 'trafficking' should not be associated with prostitution per se but only with situations that contain elements of labour abuse, for instance forced labour, slavery or servitude (Doezema, 2001; Saunders, 2000). Situations of 'trafficking' occur, therefore, when women are 'recruited' or work in conditions where force and deception have been used. Since this perspective takes prostitution to be a form of paid work and a voluntary contractual exchange between adults, its advocates distinguish between women who choose to enter prostitution and those who are forced into it and hence set apart 'voluntary' from 'forced' prostitution.

This distinction might be read in terms of a recognition of the right to self-determination of sex workers and thus a success of sex workers' organisations in displacing the abolitionist discourse of the International Human Rights Network, which defines all prostitution as invariably forced. In fact, positing sex work as a form of labour and an income-generating activity permitted advocates of sex workers' rights to contest claims that prostitution is invariably and always forced and emphasise instead that women choose sex work out of economic need and/or the feeling of control it gives them over sexual interactions (Delacoste and Alexander, 1988). It also allowed for a critique of those positions that interpret prostitution as a form of psycho- or socio-pathological deviance of individual women and, by pointing out the similarities between sex work and other types of labour, permitted sex workers' rights advocates to re-focus attention onto the struggle for improving sex workers' rights and working conditions (Pheterson, 1996).[3] However, rather than disrupting them, the differentiation between 'voluntary' and 'forced' prostitution ended up displacing onto coerced prostitution the old stereotypes and moral judgements about prostitution and, moreover, it racialised the two categories (Doezema, 1998; Murray, 1998). Consensual prostitution is assumed to be performed by Western sex workers capable of self determination, while situations of coerced prostitution are seen to affect passive and inexperienced Third World and migrant women (Kapur, 2008).[4]

The separation between coerced and consensual prostitution was also a problematic one for the International Human Rights Network but for quite different reasons than those proposed by the Human Rights Caucus. The Coalition against Trafficking in Women (CATW), the leading organisation within the International Human Rights Network, maintained what is known as a feminist abolitionist position, in which it is held that all prostitution is coerced and is the result of male oppression and dominance over women (Leidholdt, 1999). The founder of CATW, Kathleen Barry, describes prostitution as follows: 'I am taking prostitution as the model, the most extreme and most crystallized form of all sexual exploitation. Sexual exploitation is a political condition, the foundation of women's subordination and the base from which discrimination against women is constructed and enhanced' (Barry, 1995: 11). Since prostitution is part of patriarchal domination over female sexuality and its existence negatively affects all women by consolidating men's rights of access to women's bodies, for CATW the notion of self determination or consent in relation to prostitution makes little or, better, no sense at all. In fact, given that from this perspective prostitution equals sexual slavery, no woman can consent freely to her own exploitation. The International Human Rights Network activists concentrated their lobbying efforts on the notion of consent and argued for adopting a definition of trafficking that is not contingent upon the woman's consent. The line of reasoning was that this would remove the burden of proof from the victims and place it on the exploiters, hence avoiding the risk of legal discrimination between deserving and undeserving victims (Raymond, 2002: 494). While the argument concerning the burden of proof and the differentiation between victims is an extremely interesting and valid one, its potential is limited by an understanding of prostitution exclusively as violence against women and results in the impossibility of separating 'trafficking' from prostitution. It also makes it impossible to conceptualise 'trafficking' beyond the narrow frame of patriarchal domination that posits men as oppressors and sex as the tool by which men's power over women is exercised. In order to end the objectification, commodification and exploitation of women and their sexuality, abolitionist feminists support measures that penalise sex buyers and criminalise all forms of third party involvement in prostitution with the aim of ultimately eradicating prostitution all together.

The analysis of labour arrangements in third party controlled street prostitution, which I undertake in this chapter, sits uneasily with opinions that all too easily embrace the notions of consent and force as the basis for separating free and forced prostitution and identifying 'trafficking' with the latter. The reasons for this are several. First, the binary opposition between consensual versus coerced prostitution is problematic because it conceptually ties migration to 'trafficking'. As I show throughout this chapter, this association conceals similarities between migrant and non-migrant women's experiences of third party controlled street prostitution. Second, an emphasis on the coerced nature of the bond between the woman and a third party hinders the resources migrant women generate and the agency they enact despite the exploitative labour conditions and various forms of abuse that often accompany street prostitution. Furthermore, it assumes that the bond between the parties is not negotiable and that violence is both a distinguishing trait of migrant women's prostitution and is present for the whole duration of the prostitution contract. I illustrate that in taking these assumptions for granted we fail to see that the arrangements into which women entered are not unchangeable or absolute. Finally, the notion of coerced prostitution, in particular in its association with slavery, assumes that third parties wield consolidated and homogeneous domination over the women from whose labour they profit.

Instead of giving credence to the assumption that third parties exercise complete control over women's lives, in this chapter I show the complexity of relations and arrangements regulating migrant women's labour in third party controlled street prostitution. I broaden the analysis in an attempt to shift the focus from third parties as the primary cause of women's 'unfreedom' and towards a multi-layered 'condition of confinement', which, as Julia O'Connell Davidson (1998: 29) puts it, is the combination of 'conditions that prevent exit from prostitution through the use of physical restraint, physical violence or the threat thereof, or through the threat of other non-economic sanctions, such as imprisonment or deportation'. I investigate and hence unravel the conditions of confinement women experienced in third party controlled street prostitution and the modes through which these conditions were organised and maintained. I distinguish between personal and impersonal forms of control/forces and show how the personal mode of control exercised by third parties and the impersonal forces resulting from legal and economic constraints interlock to produce a situation of confinement and exploitation in prostitution. This distinction makes it possible to examine the relationships migrant women established and resources they generated, which in turn enabled them to engage, negotiate and modify their situations of confinement or leave street prostitution all together.

Personal forms of control

Starting from respondents' accounts of entry into street prostitution, this section investigates the means by which third parties constrained women's mobility and controlled their labour in order to maximise the economic gain.

Entry into street prostitution as a moment of shock

When asked to describe their experiences of arriving in Italy, the women spoke of having been shocked when first confronted with street prostitution, the difficulty of coping with the social and spatial confinement, and with the control exercised by third parties. The respondents spoke at large about the moment of their arrival at their destination, their introduction to prostitution and their first days on the street.[5] Most told of the moment of starting work on the streets and the shock this situation produced. Interestingly, the description of this initial situation of shock is present in all of the narratives, independent of whether or not women consented to working in prostitution at the time of 'recruitment'. It might appear as a contradiction that even those women who entered a sex work contract experienced shock upon arrival. The causes of shock are manifold. First, the shock stemmed from the fact that the terms of the contract between the third party and the woman were left vague: these did not specify living or working conditions, the amount of working hours or the work rate. What was explicitly agreed upon was the length of the contract, usually amounting to three months, and the payment of ten per cent of the earnings, which corresponded approximately to a sum between 1000 and 1200 EUR.[6] Simply imagining what street prostitution is actually like was the second cause for shock. Some women entertained romantic images of prostitution, such as Ioanna, who, when asked how she imagined prostitution before coming to Italy, replied: 'Like in a movie'.[7] Other women did not expect to work on the street but rather in a bar and prostitute occasionally to top up their earnings. Yet even for those women who knew that they would be working in street prostitution, it was quite a challenge to imagine themselves actually on the street, and they often felt displaced. Oksana offered an example of the confusion she went through when arriving at 'her' workplace for the first time:

> I knew I was supposed to stay outside but did not know where or how. I went there together with Sonia. I said: 'Come on, let's go. We'll find the place'. I started walking [along the street]. [There were

some houses there and I thought that] perhaps we need to enter one of the doors. Then, at the end, I said: 'No, Sonia, number 24 is here. We must stay here!?'

What Oksana describes in terms of confusion and surprise, Marisa narrates in terms of trauma and disorientation. Her feeling of powerlessness is worsened due to the fact that she did not speak any Italian:

> I started to work on the second day. I did not know the language, nothing. I felt bad. We were not used to standing like in a shop window; the client comes, looks at you, goes and fucks you ... I felt betrayed because I was selling myself for money. I could only see the street ... I was selling my body for money, for money that I could not keep. I gave all the money to the pimp.

This combination of surprise, shock, guilt, disorientation and constant pressure from a third party during those first weeks in prostitution resulted in a sensation of not being able to cope and wanting to run away. This initial period of shock was followed by a phase of resignation and of finding ways to cope with the situation. For Natasha, getting used to the confinement of street prostitution meant giving herself up to depression: 'You know [after a week] I got used to coming and going, but I did not want to think of anything. I thought that for me life has ended ... I did not care at all.' For Maja, it was a moment of shock followed by inevitable adaptation: 'I was shocked. The first time and it was on the road. ... I couldn't see anything but those cars. ... It was a shock. It was indescribable. But then I adapted. ... I got used to it.'

Another element that contributed to the initial moment of shock is spatial isolation and limitation imposed on women's movement, whether via third party control or the location. This is best conveyed through quotations such as Marisa's 'I could only see the street' or, similarly, 'I couldn't see anything but those cars' by Maja. These narrow spatial coordinates that respondents experienced upon their arrival and that revolved around the street and the residential complex nearby were in stark contrast with the expectations women entertained prior to leaving for Italy. The decision to migrate was informed by the women's desire to leave stagnant life situations behind and open up space for new economic, social and romantic opportunities. The spatial and social isolation that women faced in third party-controlled prostitution immediately upon their arrival in Italy conflicted with these women's migratory expectations and goals. Far from being able to realise their projects of mobility and autonomy, respondents had to deal with the fact that their movements and interactions were confined to the narrow spaces of prostitution. This feeling of being trapped in prostitution is typical of third party controlled street prostitution. In her study of prostitution in the Midlands, Joanna Phoenix discussed how, for the white English women she interviewed, prostitution was initially perceived as a way to escape certain men or a life on welfare and instead to lead an independent life. Yet, due to economic exploitation, physical violence and retaliations typical of the 'practice of poncing' as a structural aspect of prostitution (Phoenix, 1999: 116),[8] third party controlled street prostitution did not translate into the opening of new possibilities but rather into a trap that prevented women from living autonomous lives. For Phoenix's interviewees, 'poncing' meant accepting the idea of prostitution as a trap that could not be escaped.

These feelings of entrapment and resignation mirror the descriptions of immobility during the initial period in third party prostitution expressed by women in my study. As for Phoenix's interviewees, my respondents' feeling of entrapment was an effect of constraints imposed on their mobility by third parties and of the violence these third parties used to control women's performance in prostitution. However, my data also indicate that third party's use of violence was not a permanent occurrence but it rather took place immediately upon women's arrival in Italy. The first days in prostitution were those when power hierarchies were made clear. Marisa, after she was told what she was required to do, for whom and how, understood that she was momentarily not in a position to negotiate her situation: 'I remained silent; I could not say much. I had just arrived in Italy and he could do with me whatever he pleased'. What we can observe, therefore, is that the initial moment of shock and disorientation, followed by the period of adaptation and resignation, intensified women's feeling of immobility. These all worked in favour of third parties who, exactly during this initial moment of confusion, set in motion a number of strategies aimed at establishing control over women's labour.

Physical violence and the threat thereof

The threat of violence is the predominant form of control that third parties used to secure power over women. Third parties often threatened to use physical violence against women or to impinge on their basic needs by such means as depriving them of food. Some women were frightened by this treatment while others who had had previous experience of the sex industry took it as a 'normal' dynamic: 'Of course, they shouted and screamed, "What is this? If there is no work [no clients], you'll work twenty-four hours a day, and won't eat"'. Asserting that the threat of violence is the most present form of control is not to suggest that third parties did not resort to physical violence at all. On the contrary, several women were left injured as a result of third parties' direct physical violence. For example, Ioanna and Oksana had a five-month contract for sex work with an Albanian man. Contrary to the majority of other respondents, they enjoyed relative freedom of movement. The two women lived in a hotel in the centre of Bologna and prostituted on the nearby streets. They did not see the third party on a daily basis as he came to the hotel only once a week to collect money. After ten days of prostitution it became clear that the third party had a different image of the contract than the respondents. He dogged them on their way to and from work, objected to their going to dinner with clients and claimed that they did not earn enough. After threatening the respondents with a beating, he used physical violence first against one and then against the other respondent, causing concussion to one of them. He also threatened to shoot the same respondent in the legs.

While acts of violence need to be acknowledged, it is equally important to remark that physical violence seems to be time bound, namely that third parties used violence predominantly immediately after women's arrival in Italy. Later they seem to maintain control not through violence but rather through the threat of violence. We can see this best in the case of Ivana, who was hit on the head by a male third party causing her hearing damage when she refused to work in prostitution. From then on, the third party did not use physical violence but maintained control through the constant threat of violence. A female pimp would tell Ivana how violent her male pimp-partner was and how he hurt other women under his control. At the same time, the male pimp would tell similar stories about his female partner. Following this initiation to the 'rules of the game', third parties were less present and passed the maintenance of control to others, usually women who had in the past been in the same position as Ivana but now principally maintained control over 'new' girls and did sex work only occasionally.

Even if women did not experience physical violence from third parties, they were aware that others around them did and felt that the same might happen to them. Other scholars studying migrant women's prostitution in Italy reached similar conclusions and showed that third parties usually increase their use of violence or threaten violence at the moment of women's entry to prostitution in order to gain control over labour and assert control and power (Carchedi, 2003: 130–1; Maluccelli,

2001: 50–1). It is also important to observe that physical violence and threats are not characteristic exclusively of migrant women's street prostitution but rather of third party controlled street work in general. Contrary to sex work away from the streets, such as in saunas or clubs, third party controlled street prostitution is inherently characterised by a high degree of violence (McKeganey and Barnard, 1996; O'Neill, 2001; Phoenix, 1999). There is little distinction between the use of, or the threat to use, violence in non-migrant pimp-controlled street prostitution compared to migrant street prostitution. Rather than being a peculiar characteristic of migrant women's situation, third parties' use of (or threat of) violence to establish control and command over prostitutes seems to be a typical feature of third party controlled street prostitution in general.

Non-violent forms of control

Third party controlled street prostitution may rely on surveillance and control of women's movements as a way of establishing power over women's labour. Third parties controlled women's movements by organising their housing in such a way that women had to share their living space with third parties or with other women working for the same third party. Women's accommodation varied between a hotel room, a private house/apartment, or a large private six-floor housing complex on the outskirts of the city of Bologna known as the Calderara Residence. Those women placed in a hotel usually shared a room with a peer worker or with the 'pimp'. For those sharing a room with a peer worker this meant that they could rest after a night of work and claim that space as theirs. For those who lived in the same room as the third party, sharing the same space meant being additionally exposed to the third party's control and requests. For Larisa, whose pimp was a man, sharing accommodation with the third party involved handling his sexual advances. Larisa tried to manage the situation by offering the third party 25 EUR, the standard prostitution fee for sexual services in a car, in order for him to leave her alone and instead go to the street and have intercourse with another woman. However, he would refuse saying that he was in love with her and that he desired only her. For Larisa, living with the third party meant ongoing negotiations regarding sexual access to her person. At times, she was successful; at other times she was not.

When women lived in private apartments or houses with a group of their peers and third parties, those apartments were usually quite distant from the place on the street where they worked and so they travelled collectively either by train or in a third party's car. Those respondents who lived in the Residence and prostituted in the area not far away faced a very similar situation. They were allowed to move only between the Residence and the street, and were forbidden to socialise with clients and women working for other third parties. Natasha describes it like this: 'One goes out to the street each night but cannot even go for a stroll, or in a bar to drink something'. What we see then is third party's direct or indirect control of women's movement and actions. Direct control entailed the third party's being physically present on the street and checking on women. The most common form of indirect control meant that the third party would drive by or ring the women to check on their location and working schedule. Third parties equipped the women with mobile phones specifically to allow them to call and check on them, giving the impression of being nearby while not being anywhere near the place. I refer to this in terms of the 'illusion of control' because third parties were often actually not present physically but had the ability to check on women through mobile phones or other prostitutes. Routinely, third parties relied on women themselves to inform them of the whereabouts of others. This created a situation of distrust between women. As Ester put it: 'One fears saying anything because if you tell one of the other girls that you have money she will tell the pimp. There was a kind of jealousy among us. One feared oneself. You did not know ... you slept in the same bed but still you were scared of her.' In a similar manner, another respondent describes the situation of jealousy and competition within the group of other migrant women she was living and working with:

> The pimp would not be there next to you to hear what you are saying. The problem was that the other girls would listen to your conversations and would tell him that you do not do this, you do not do that, or that you refused a client because he is ugly or old. Among the girls, the one who would make most money, namely the one who cheated the best, the one who was the toughest, the strongest ... in order to be the pimp's favourite, she would show that she is better then the others. This was totally wrong because the pimp would not pay any of us: neither the one who did a lot nor the one who did little.

Kateryna's description of the constant surveillance highlights the ways in which third parties indirectly maintained control via a system based on suspicion and competition among women. Research on both independent street sex work as well as sex work in clubs and bars by non-migrant women has shown that women are often in competition or suspicious of each other, that friendships between them are transitory, and that at times they also assault each other physically (Brennan, 2004; Nencel, 2000; McKeganey and Barnard, 1996). My findings may explain why what Phoenix called the 'institution of prostitution' leads to the fabrication of and investment into heterosexual emotional dependence, which in combination with women's economic needs and competition among women, favours individualism and averts sex workers' collective organising (Phoenix, 1999).

Condition of confinement and economic exploitation

In addition to the forms of constraint described above, women's movement and social interaction was also regulated by the working schedule, working rate and various degrees of economic pressure. The working rate consisted of approximately 12 clients per shift[9], with shifts being an eight-hour per night. Third parties attempted to limit women's encounters with clients to 15 minutes, during which time it was expected that they drive to a parking area, perform the agreed service and drive back. This imposing of time-limits on women-client interactions was due to the fact that for the third party it was easier to control women's movements once they were back standing on the street. Limiting physical movement and social interaction among women, as well as between women and clients, also aimed at preventing the flow of information between the parties, as information could enable women to exit the situation of confinement. An excerpt from Kateryna's interview points to the fact that she was aware of the potential offered by social interaction with clients: 'We could not go out with the clients and go and eat something together, not even during the day, because the pimp said that we would talk, that the client would tell you things and that you would suddenly wake up and leave. They could not allow this to happen'. As this quotation summarises so well, third parties attempted to limit the interaction between women and clients since it was likely to offer the migrant women an insight into the world from which they were deliberately being kept out.

Quite clearly, in the case where a woman leaves, the third party's sources of earnings lessen. A quote from Marisa's narrative addresses this subject:

> They [pimps] fear to lose [the women]. They do not care how much money they get but how much they do not get. This is why they are scared to lose the girls. One [of the female pimps I knew] had three girls and two of them left. Do you know how much she cried because of it? A friend of mine had a problem and she wanted to

make some money in order to buy a flat, a house. When she was left with only one girl, she started to cry and said: 'What do I do with one girl only? I must immediately buy other girls.'

So third parties impose control on migrant women's mobility and labour in prostitution predominantly because they are scared of 'losing' their labour force and therefore their own source of income. Using a variety of strategies and means of control, third parties aim at profiting from women's labour and generating the most profit in the shortest time possible. From the examination of the 'contract' between the third parties and respondents, it emerges that the third parties' goal, independent of whether they were women or men, was to achieve a maximum profit by controlling the rate of prostitute-client exchanges and making sure that women surrender all of their earnings, or to put it differently that they keep as little money as possible. Third parties, my analysis suggests, made use of migrant labour because this population was driven by economic need, unfamiliar with the surroundings and did not master the language spoken in the destination country.

Keeping in mind that women serviced a large number of clients per night and that those interactions are for the most part out of a third party's reach, it is simply an illusion that a third party might be able to fully control women's social interaction. By gathering information and observing the 'rules' of the game, women generated resources that enabled them to exit third party controlled prostitution and work independently or quit sex work all together. Women inevitably got acquainted with the local situation both in terms of learning how the system works and of how to take advantage of it themselves. In order to establish control and power over women during this initial period, third parties manipulated women's initial feeling of shock, restrained their social interactions and physical mobility and fabricated a situation of (emotional) dependence. In time, this initial abusive situation was transformed to give space to a less violent and more consensual relationship between the women and the third party, which remained geared nevertheless towards maximising the earnings generated by women's labour (Carchedi, 2003; Maluccelli, 2001).

Impersonal forms of control

While much attention is paid to personal forms of control, the impersonal forces that confine women to street prostitution are frequently overlooked. In what follows, I examine the impersonal forces, such as

economic and legal constraints, that are equally important to understanding how conditions of confinement are facilitated, created and
sustained. I focus on the degree of financial need among respondents,
'debt bondage' and immigration and labour regulations as three key
factors.

Economic Pressure

The desire to improve one's own or one's family's economic situation
strongly influenced women's migratory projects. Yet, next to being a
motivator for achieving mobility or autonomy, economic need also
had the opposite effect and at times played a key role in sustaining the
conditions of confinement. This was certainly the case for Ester and
Tatiana. The first time Ester arrived in Italy she found out that the nursing job she was promised was a fake. After a couple of weeks spent in
third party controlled street prostitution, she ran away and returned to
Moldova. Some months later she and her sister left for Italy with the
promise of domestic work and ended up in prostitution near Bologna
instead. While the first time on the street was a great shock to Ester, the
second time she was more familiar with the environment and kept a
close eye on the third parties in order to get an idea of their movements
and plan her and her sister's escape. Unfortunately, her plans failed
when her father became sick and her mother needed her to send money
home for medications and hospitalisation. When she first learned of her
father's illness, Ester tried to pressure the third party to let her and her
sister return to Moldova. The third party refused but she managed to
negotiate for her sister Tatiana to return to Moldova. Ester found herself
in a situation of great economic pressure as, on the one hand, the third
party pressured her to work in order to repay the debt she and her sister
contracted in order to reach Italy and, on the other, her mother kept on
demanding that she send money home. Ester described it like this:

> I would do everything possible to send money home. They [my
> mum and sister] called me when I would not [call them]. There were
> moments when I could not take any money … and then my mum
> would phone me; she called me to help her. To make her sleep at
> night I would from time to time even send her 25 EUR paying the
> transfer fees on the top. This because my father needed medicines
> urgently the very same day. I would also ask clients: 'Can you give
> me something? Give me 50 EUR'. Then I would divide it: 25 for me
> and 25 for the pimp. At home, they needed money from one day to
> the other. When phoning home and talking with my mum, I fought

back my tears. I would talk to her and fight back my tears in order not to cry.

The need to send money home meant that Ester could not yet leave third party controlled prostitution.

Similarly, economic need was the reason why some other women returned to do sex work. Ana, for example, got help from a client shortly upon her arrival in Italy, left third party-controlled street prostitution and was hosted by two religious institutions that functioned as shelters for 'trafficked' women. She got kicked out of the first one on the accusation of having had sexual intercourse[10] and left the second one because she felt it was like a prison. However, walking out of there put her in a difficult situation, first, because she was illegal and vulnerable to deportation and, second, because she had no place to live and no money for food. Ana therefore took up the offer from a Moldovan woman while she was staying at the religious shelter:

> She came to me and immediately she asked in Italian 'Where do you come from?' 'From Moldova' [I answered] and from there on I started talking in Moldavian. We chatted and I said 'Look, I feel ill at ease here: I do not know what I am doing here' and she answered 'I can help you with the flat but then you need to go back to the street. You can work for yourself but you need to pay 25 EUR a day for the flat'. So, I had no other choice because I knew that if I stayed there nothing would happen. I had to do something, do you understand? I thought, maybe I will be lucky this time. And so, I stayed [in the flat], I lived there. I worked for myself: when I wanted I went to work and when no, I did not. I would work only during the night for three to four hours, not more. That was enough to pay for food and for some clothes. In the meantime I always tried to meet people.

Returning to sex work was for Ana at the same time both the continuation and postponement of her migration project. Having no other economic prospects, she opted for prostitution and thus postponed her plans to stay in Italy and support herself through something other than sex work. However, even though she needed to suspend her project momentarily, at the same time she was determined to carry it through and did so by attempting to get to know as many clients as possible who could help her find alternative work ('I always tried to meet people').

A similar situation of economic need was faced by Sasha who had a relationship with an ex client, an Italian man, who left her after she got pregnant and refused to have an abortion. Faced with the situation of having no man to support her and having no money or place to live on her own, Sasha returned to sex work and worked independently. Contrary to when she just arrived in Italy and lived and worked with a group of women who, after the third party they all worked for got arrested, got organised and paid the rent collectively, this time she had to do it on her own. She organised her work to make as much money in as little time as possible, working each night from 9 pm until 5–6 am. She managed to save on rent money because a friend let her use her apartment. After three months, Sasha stopped doing sex work after having put aside 6000 EUR, the amount she thought would cover her and her child's costs for a while.

Economic pressure from families and women's need to secure money for basic necessities are reasons that tied migrant women to third party controlled prostitution or why some respondents returned to do independent sex work. In this respect, respondents' experiences resemble the accounts of non-migrant women since in both cases 'women prostitute to make money' (McKeganey and Barnard, 1996) or take up sex work as a short-term survival strategy to meet their obligations as single mothers (Brennan, 2004: 120). While the debate on 'trafficking' stresses that women are not paid any money, my data suggests that some women were paid the agreed sum at the end of a three-month contract period. Others managed to gain money through tips from clients, by hiding a part of the earnings from third parties, or by being given, by the third party, a sum of money to send home. The amount of money respondents obtained differed greatly, but nevertheless sex work allowed women access to money whether under third party control or the women's independent management. These considerations also call into question the assumption that women are bound to the third party through the debt they contract. As the case of Ester shows, the main condition that sustained her confinement to third party-controlled street prostitution was not her and her sister's debt but the economic pressure her mother put her under. In fact, she had escaped the control of another third party once already and did so again immediately after her father passed away.

Debt bondage

In mainstream studies of third party controlled prostitution, debt is invoked as the 'norm in the world of traffickers and their victims' and the means by which third parties transform a woman into a 'prisoner of debt bondage' (Shannon, 1999: 123) and leave women 'obligated *indefinitely* to their employers' (emphasis mine) (Caldwell et al., 1999: 63). The assumption that debt lasts for an indefinite period of time has been disputed by studies of indoor sex work conducted in Australia, Canada, Germany and Japan. These have shown that debt bondage is limited to the period of the repayment and that once the debt has been settled, women were able to keep their income (Meaker, 2002; Ratanaloan Mix, 2002; Sutdhibhasilp, 2002). Researchers have also examined different logic upholding the debt-bondage by contextualising the various systems of debt within the local economies or religious traditions (Aoyama, 2009; Phongpaichit, 1999).

Yet placing an emphasis on debt per se can lead to an 'illusion of similitude' and fail to take sufficient account of the different kinds of social relations prostitution involves. As Alan Knight (1988: 103) pointed out in his historical study of debt bondage in Latin America, 'the mere fact of debt, which is the overt feature of debt peonage, may ... create an illusory similitude among forms of labour which differ radically in respect of subjective conditions/perceptions and objective social implications'. While existing literature on debt-bonded prostitution has shown that the presence of debt binds women to third parties for a determinate period of time, it is interesting that women in my study made little reference to the need to repay the debt they contracted.[11] Exceptions are those women who borrowed an exact amount of money to pay for the travel and the visa and who were aware that they had to pay back this loan. Others did not refer to the obligation to repay the contracted debt but if they mentioned debt at all they did so to emphasise the pressure they were under. While it might seem that debt is an important factor in enhancing the conditions of confinement, most respondents did not see debt as a factor preventing them from exiting the situation of confinement. I am not suggesting that debt played no role at all but that women were not too worried about whether they would be able to settle the debt or not and did not perceive themselves as 'bound' to a third party by that debt.

Let me illustrate this through an example. After a long journey through the Balkans, Larisa was brought to Italy to prostitute by a young Albanian man. She was aware that he had invested money in her, paid for all of her travel and subsistence and made it possible for her to come to Italy. However, this did not prevent her from running away from him after two weeks in Italy. In doing so she was helped by a friend from the same home town who worked previously in third party controlled street prostitution and who stayed in Italy once she exited sex work. Without the Albanian man knowing, the friend picked her up from the street and struck a deal with Larisa to work for her. After a month of sex work, Larisa did not manage to keep any money for herself as all of her earnings were spent on the hotel room, food and the fee for the new third party. Having not earned anything, she was not motivated to work any longer and decided to quit. When commenting on this episode Larisa remarked: 'She was stupid, really really stupid because she took me from the street. I came to Italy alone, so to say: she paid no money for me'. What Larisa means is that the woman incurred no costs as she was not the one who brought her to Italy and that they could have divided the earnings more equally.[12] Interestingly, Larisa omits the fact that she was brought to Italy by the Albanian man and says instead that she 'arrived on her own, so to say'. The 'so to say' phrase is the point at which the story is altered. What are the reasons for this narrative reversal? Viewed within the complexity of the respondent's entire narrative, this shift points to the personal investment Larisa made into her migratory project. She is aware that her arrival in Italy was made possible by a third party from Albania but, at the same time, she frames it within her own struggle to leave Moldova and reach Italy. The third party is someone who does constrain and abuse her but he is also perceived as a means by which she has arrived at the desired destination. Whereas he might think that she owes him money as he advanced funds to get her to Italy, she sees that money not as her debt but rather as his investment and personal risk. This did not reverse the power hierarchy between the woman and third parties but it does suggest that there is a need to research more closely the nature of the debt in so called 'debt-bonded prostitution' and the factors that sustain a condition of confinement. Against the idea that third parties keep women indefinitely, my study suggests that, for third parties, the possibility of 'holding' a woman for a certain period of time in order to exploit her labour, appropriate her earnings and maximise economic gain is more relevant and more profitable than the repayment of the debt per se (Bales, 2000: 18).

Unlike the more formal systems of indenture used to recruit migrant sex workers in South East Asia for example (Phongpaichit, 1999), respondents did not know the exact amount of money they owed to a third party as the amount was rarely specified. Some scholars argue that the fact that a third party debits a certain sum to the migrants in a non-transparent way facilitates migrants' economic exploitation. This is because the indebted never knows how much debt she has managed to pay back and how much she still has left to settle (Carchedi, 2003; Bales, 2000). I would like to put forward a different interpretation: the lack of transparency and exact specification of debt might also work in the women's favour since the elusiveness surrounding the debt can diminish the importance women ascribe to it and thus the pressure on the debtor by the lender. The existence of the debt need not in itself constitute a condition of confinement. This needs to be examined in particular in relation to the data produced by this and other studies that show that it is not uncommon for migrant women to leave third party controlled prostitution (Della Giusta et al., 2008: 67). Additionally, if women had to pay third parties for each illegal crossing of the border or had to pay high visa fees, the debate on debt needs to move away from focusing exclusively on third parties and include an analysis of restrictive immigration and border and visa regimes as factors that facilitate and sustain indebtedness and unfree labour relations.

The role of the state

If border and visa regimes rendered women vulnerable to abuse and exploitation during the cross-border journey, the residency and labour regulations in Italy exacerbated this situation even further. Because in Italy prostitution is not considered work, it is not covered by labour legislation and legal immigration status cannot be acquired by means of independent earnings within the sex trade. Even in cases where this is possible, as for example in the Netherlands, the respondents would have not been eligible as most of them came from countries not included in the *European Agreements on the Right of Establishment* which grant the nationals of the Central and Eastern European countries the right to self employment in the EU. Independent of the type of work they agreed to do, what is common to all women is that they made work arrangements with third parties rather than via official state-run channels, such as consulates, responsible for entry and work visas. Some women therefore entered the EU undocumented while others became illegal having overstayed their visa. This means that independent of how they initially entered Italy, most of the women's immigration status during their stay in the sex trade was that of an illegal migrant.

Being illegal impacted respondents' lives in significant ways: it limited their labour options to the 'informal' sectors and, more precisely, to the care and the sex sectors. As migrant women's work in the care sector is notoriously underpaid, those women who were faced with an urgent economic need turned to the sex sector and returned to working in independent or third party controlled street prostitution. Next to severely limiting women's possibility to change type of work, being illegal exposed women to arrest and deportation. It is common for migrant women working under third party control in street prostitution to get arrested, sent to a detention centre for undocumented migrants and then deported (Pearson, 2002; Sossi, 2002). In this case, women were not eligible for the next five years for an EU visa and, if determined to enter the EU, could do so only via illegal channels. Moreover, Italian Immigration Law has recently been revised since the government found it to be too permissive. A new clause was introduced, which considers illegal entry into Italy a criminal offence. If, after deportation, a person re-enters Italy undocumented, she/he could be punished with six months to five years in prison and then deported again.

Similar to other undocumented migrants, the fear of deportation prevented women from seeking help from the police (Sutdhibhasilp, 2002; Wijers and Lap-Chew, 1997). The police were the last resource women considered and they would contact them only after having run out of other options. Kateryna and Daniela, for example, ran away from a third party's control and wanted to stay in Italy, but in order to do so needed to convince the third party to return Daniela's passport to her. When all of their attempts to get hold of the passport failed and they did not know what to do next, they went to the police accepting the fact that they would get deported:

> This situation could not go on like this. I could not return home because I had no money, but she didn't even have a passport. They [the police] will stop her at the border and she will be in loads of trouble. So, what were we to do? We could not even go back home! ... I knew one could press charges, but I had no idea that one could get a permit to stay. I knew nothing of it. What I knew was that if I go to the police to press charges they will ship me back home.

This situation played into hands of third parties and contributed significantly to sustaining conditions of confinement. That immigration status has a key role in constructing situations of vulnerability and exploitation is confirmed by other studies in Spain, Portugal and the UK. The study of indoor prostitution in the border region of Spain and Portugal found that these establishments employ mostly undocumented migrant women from Latin America. Due to their illegal status, women tend to keep a low profile, they rarely exit their accommodation or club and have few social interactions outside the work environment as they fear being apprehended by the police and deported. This gives club owners more control over women's time and labour and this claustrophobic situation feeds into interpersonal conflicts with other prostitutes. It also further contains women to the circles of sex work as, in trying to remain undetected by the authorities, women tend to rotate between clubs and develop only short-term attachments (Ribeiro and Sacramento, 2005). A study of the migrant UK indoor sex industry found immigration status by far the single most important factor restricting migrants' ability to improve their professional and personal lives. Being undocumented at times restricted migrants' employment choices to such an extent that migrants viewed the sex sector to be the only safe option as it did not involve moving in public spaces and hence reduced the fear of arrest and deportation (Mai, 2009). These research results call for consideration of the arguments that the sex sector needs to be more closely state regulated. The shift to prostitution as a legalised type of work is likely to secure rights and give more protection to EU citizens but not to undocumented non-EU nationals for whom more visibility will mean more risk of arrest and deportation (O'Connell Davidson, 2006).

The illegal status also exposed women to additional forms of abuse. For example, since undocumented migrants are not allowed to open bank accounts, women kept their earnings on them and suffered attacks by clients who attempted to steal their money or by third parties if they discovered that women did not surrender all of their earnings. Being charged an exorbitant rent fee was also the consequence of being undocumented. At the housing complex, called the Calderara Residence, where a number of women were staying, the rent one had to pay depended on immigration status. Migrants with papers were charged 400 EUR per month, but undocumented migrants had to pay 800 EUR per month for the same space. This situation, in which women were exposed to detention and deportation by the state and to profiting from various intermediaries, enhanced women's dependency on third parties for work and living arrangements and consigned women to a situation of heightened third party control. In their report on 'trafficking', Anti-Slavery International remarked that third parties 'manipulate the isolation and vulnerability of trafficked persons and use and exploit current legal systems, especially the migration laws, to further marginalise and exploit trafficked persons' (Pearson, 2002: 43). However, what the report fails to mention but which needs to be remarked upon and included in any analysis of 'trafficking' is that the decisions that third parties make concerning labour practices depends upon particular legal contexts. By this I mean that a combination of restrictive residency and labour regulations increases migrants' vulnerability and dependence on a third party, restrains women's social and labour mobility and reinforces the personal type of control that facilitates third party exploitation of migrant women's labour in prostitution. Irregular migrants find themselves in a situation in which they have little choice but to accept extremely exploitative employment arrangements and poor working conditions. The role of the state and its immigration regulations needs therefore to feature in any analysis of how the conditions of exploitation and abuse of migrant labour are maintained and perpetuated.

To sum up, let us recall that the condition of 'trafficked' women party controlled is commonly identified as unique and exceptional due to the high level of abuse and violence that third parties use to keep women under their control. However, my analysis has shown that the control and abuse migrant women experience is neither unique to the situation of 'trafficked' women, nor can third parties be identified as the only source of dominance and power. In order to maintain control over the women they exploit, third parties use a series of violent and non-violent forms of control, all geared towards maximising the economic gain generated by women's labour. Again, this situation cannot be identified as specific to migrant women. Rather, it is characteristic of third party controlled street prostitution in general. The particularity of the situation of confinement experienced by migrant women lies in the overlap produced by the control exercised by third parties and the control the Italian state and the EU exercises over migrants' mobility and labour via restrictive immigration and employment regulations. It is the fear of deportation and the impossibility to access other forms of work due to limits imposed by residency and employment laws that plays a crucial role in confining migrant women to prostitution and, in turn, in increasing the women's dependency on a controlling third party.

Exits: Resources generated in prostitution

In this section I discuss the type of resources women generated while working in third party controlled street prostitution that consequently enabled them to exit sex work. In the previous section I gave an account of the conditions of confinement that women experienced and suggested that, while physical violence might have been used against women during their initial period in prostitution, as time passed these instances of physical violence or threats thereof became replaced by what I called the 'illusion of control'. Since third parties quite often profited from the labour of a group of women that might be as large as eight, it was impossible for them to be physically present at all times, keep constant control, or prevent interaction among women or between women and clients. These factors allowed respondents to create a limited space in which to engender a number of resources via negotiations with third parties, police, other sex workers and clients leading to an improvement in their working and living arrangements. To describe these relationships I borrow the term 'bond' from O'Connell Davidson (1998) as this term fittingly conveys the situation of interdependency as well as the asymmetrical power relations that sustained them.

The third parties

Third party organisers of prostitution, as I discussed in Chapter 2, do not exert total control over women. They are not all men, as it is often assumed due to the emphasis placed on sexual slavery, and they do not adopt the same approach to conducting business. Far from being absent, women featured regularly as a third party and were predominantly involved in running 'recruitment' agencies, organising transportation and controlling respondents' work in street prostitution. When third parties are not subsumed under the homogeneous category of 'traffickers', it is possible to detect different types of task distribution and arrangements that regulated the bond between third parties and respondents. The nature of these bonds could represent an obstacle or a resource for respondents and played an important role in their staying or leaving street prostitution.

Let me illustrate this through two contrasting examples. Oksana was part of a large group of women who entered into a (verbal) prostitution contract with two Yugoslav men. Third parties did not use physical force against Oksana or the rest of the group but relied instead on a system of fines and rewards. They set the work rate to 15 clients per night shift.[13] If the woman managed to sell sex to 20 clients, she received a piece of golden jewellery as a present. When the woman made a mistake that caused problems to the functioning of the whole group, she got publicly fined. This kind of non-violent, though manipulative bond allowed the respondent to earn 3600 USD for a three-month period and for the third party to generate high earnings without having to replace any women as none ran away. Quite in contrast to Oksana's situation, Ioanna entered into a prostitution 'contract' with a third party thinking of it as an employment arrangement. The lack of fulfilment of the terms of the contract from the third party's side and his abusive physical force resulted in Ioanna's breaking off the contract and leaving. Ioanna explains it like this: 'In my life no one ever hit me. If I work for a person and if I bring him quite some money, I do not want that person to hit me. It is not that this person needs to hug me. It is enough if I am given a place to sleep and food to eat. But he must not hit me.' The exploitative and violent nature of the bond with the third party encouraged the respondent to leave the arrangement after 20 days.

The bond between a third party and a woman might also constitute a resource for her to exit a situation of confinement and exploitation. Kateryna was recruited into sex work by her male lover from Romania. He travelled with her to Italy where she was met by his female (ex) lover who supervised women's work in prostitution. This overlap of (ex) lovers caused various scenes of jealousy and at times violent conflict between the two women. It finally resulted in a somewhat atypical arrangement: the female third party did not impose the same type of confinement on Kateryna as she did on the other five women she controlled. She allowed Kateryna to see and spend time with clients outside her working hours and off the street. She also did not keep Kateryna's passport as she did with other women and perhaps indirectly encouraged Kateryna to leave.

That the nature of the bond between women and a third party is open to negotiation and can change in favour of the woman is best shown in the case of Marisa. Upon her arrival in Italy Marisa was 'sold' to a 19-year-old woman from Moldova who was in a relationship with a male third party. The respondent realised that the two had an abusive relationship and that the woman was secretly stealing money from the man. She also found out that the female pimp wanted to leave the 'business' and was planning to 'sell' her to someone else. In exchange for letting her go, Marisa revealed to the woman where the male pimp was hiding money procured through selling drugs. This exchange made it possible for the female third party to leave with 20,000 EUR in cash and for Marisa to exit the condition of confinement and prostitute on her own. What we can observe here is that, while the bond between a third party and a woman is certainly an asymmetrical power relationship, it need not be violent and can be open to negotiation. It is a much more complex type of arrangement sustained by both economic and non-economic factors and a shifting set of relationships which warrant further study.

The police

The predominant attitude of respondents towards the police is that of mistrust. This is mainly due to the fear of deportation. Third parties took advantage of this situation and told women not to trust the police because the police will return them home without any earnings. As legal information was not available to the respondents, they were not aware of the possibility to obtain state protection for VoTs. This lack of information increased the women's vulnerability:

> He brought me by force to his place. But why [didn't I react]? Because if I screamed, I feared the police. Why did I not press charges? Because I was scared of the police: I did not know the law and I was scared that if I go to them they will send me back home to Moldova.

Illegal status and a fear of deportation made Ana vulnerable to a client's violence. After first kidnapping her, the client brought the respondent to his home, raped her, and kept her in captivity for some weeks. While third parties certainly manipulated women's fear of deportation, it is also important to note that the women were well aware that third parties equally feared apprehension by the police. If arrested, women were instructed to say that they work independently because, while prostitution is legal in Italy, the systematic organisation of prostitution by third parties is not and is punishable by law. Any contact the woman made with police was viewed with suspicion. For example, when Ester was physically abused by a client, the police, who happened to be on the spot, encouraged her to come to the police station and to make a written statement. When Ester returned from the police station, she was looked at suspiciously both by her peers and the pimp. Similarly, following the murder of a friend and peer worker, Marisa was approached and questioned by the police. When she returned home, she found that someone had ransacked her apartment. She speculated that other prostitutes had done this because they believed she had collaborated with the police and therefore 'sold out'.

However, the narratives of Ioanna, Oksana and Marisa demonstrate that women overcame the feeling of mistrust towards the police when they felt sufficiently endangered. Ioanna and Oksana worked for a third party and Marisa worked independently, but all three found themselves in life-threatening situations caused, on the one hand, by threats from third parties and, on the other, by risks posed by collaborating with the police. Ioanna and Oksana pressed charges against the third party and Marisa was approached by the police following a murder. In exchange for collaboration with the police and returning to prostitution to enable the police to catch the third party in the act of collecting their earnings, the respondents were first offered and subsequently negotiated the possibility of staying in Italy and legalising their status. Women established mutually beneficial bonds with the police and contrary to the situation in Cambodia, Bangladesh and India (Pattanaik, 2002), they were not afraid of being physically assaulted by the police but rather of being detained and deported.

Relationships with peer workers

Research on relationships between women in street prostitution has shown that relationships between peer workers are both communal and supportive and competitive and vicious (Brennan, 2004; McKeganey and Barnard, 1996; Nencel, 2000). In the second section of this chapter, I discussed some of the dynamics among women and pointed out that third parties manipulated feelings of mistrust, jealousy and competition that women felt towards their peers in order to strengthen their control over women. But relationships and friendships between women need also to be considered in their constituting an important positive resource for women. Oksana's and Ioanna's narrative supports this. The two women came from the same village in Ukraine and were friends for quite a while before coming to Italy together. The third party manipulated this friendship and used to threaten Oksana with violence by saying that he would beat up Ioanna if she did not earn more. In this way, he pressured Oksana to feel responsible for both of them and also for the injuries he might cause Ioanna. While at times this friendship created a degree of vulnerability, it was at the same time also a crucial resource because it helped them to support each other, which is rather uncommon in street prostitution (McKeganey and Barnard, 1996; Nencel, 2000: 219). Ioanna puts it like this: 'Here is not our home; we are in a foreign land. There is only me and her. If we do not help each other, no one else will.'

Relationships between peer workers who were not necessarily friends were nonetheless vital when it came to the introduction of safety and survival strategies on the street, safe sex practices and minimising the risk of clients' violence. Women gained access to such information via other women and not via third parties. Only one of the respondents indicated that she was instructed by a third party about how to sell and practise safe sex. Other women started to work without having been given any instructions except how to recognise different banknotes and pronounce 'hundred' and 'fifty'.[14] Maja described her arrival to the street and said that the third party told her nothing:

> She [the pimp] didn't tell us anything. The girls were saying that the clients may take girls to [bad] places and that one has to use her strength and not just to sit in a car and look at him. To write down the license plate. When he locks you in a car and begins to threaten you in a car or something like that, how to stop the car, where the stick shift is, how to open the door, different kinds of getting away from him, how to hurt him. But the boss doesn't give that information; the girls say that.

The information passed between women on matters of safety is at the heart of communal relationships between women in third party-controlled street prostitution. Absence of this kind of communal support can seriously endanger a woman's health and safety, as is shown by a respondent who was exploited by a couple. Ivana experienced a condition of confinement that was maintained through a constant threat of violence. She had no contact with other prostitutes working up or down the street from her and had received scarce instructions from the female 'pimp' about prostitute-client interaction. Moreover, the female third party told Ivana that she did not need to worry about condoms because it was a common practice not to use them. Ivana took what the third party said for granted. There are at least three explanations for why Ivana trusted the pimp. First, Ivana was totally unfamiliar with the work of prostitution or with issues around sexually transmitted diseases. Married and with two children of her own, she believed it impossible that she could get a STD because the vast majority of her clients were married. Second, Ivana was unfamiliar with her surroundings and even though she wanted to go to the pharmacy and buy some condoms she did know where the pharmacy was. Third, she knew that the female third party had previously worked as a prostitute herself and might have believed that she was experienced in the matter of how things work on the street.

Since Ivana was the only one working for this third party and was kept separate from other women working nearby, she had no alternative sources of information. One might think that the clients would provide this information, but this was not the case. The clients asked her simply if she was healthy and then proceeded to buy sexual services from her.[15] When the third party had to go away for a few days to arrange the arrival of a new woman from Russia, she handed control over Ivana to another woman who had worked for her in the past. The respondent was now finally able to have a conversation with two Russian women working next to her on the street, and realised that other women used condoms and that the work rate imposed on her was exorbitantly high. Having learned about Ivana's working conditions, the two Russian women told her that she should press charges against the third party and accompanied Ivana to the police station. As a consequence of getting in touch with two other sex workers, Ivana realised that she had been exploited and broke her bond with the third party.[16] Relationships between women therefore equipped women with basic survival skills such as how to cope with clients' violence or protect themselves from STDs and constituted an important resource for leaving exploitative labour arrangements in third party controlled prostitution.

Clients

Studies of street prostitution showed that among all sex workers, street workers are most at risk and that violence by clients is widespread (Corso and Landi, 1998; Phoenix, 1999; Scambler and Scambler, 1997). Name-calling, physical assault (beating and gun assault), rape and murder are 'commonplace' and 'represent the backdrop to the women's work' (McKeganey and Barnard, 1996: 70–2). Women in my study experienced very similar situations to non-migrant women working in street prostitution and developed similar strategies to minimise the risk of clients' violence, as portrayed by Ester:

> There was this one guy with a hat. I went into the car and he has his hand close to the hat. I was immediately suspicious. He was asking me: 'Where is your working-place?' And then: 'Let's go somewhere else.' And I told him 'Turn right here' and he kept on going straight and I realized that something is wrong. I grabbed his hand that was to take the hat and there was a knife hidden underneath. I took the knife and said: 'You bring me back immediately or I will kill you' I was scared but I did not know it; I was stronger then him. 'Will you take me back?' He took me back. He said: 'Are you nuts? I used this knife at my work. I just came from work.' I said: 'Yeaaahhh, at work! And you keep it here; you need to put it in the boot, why did you keep it here?'

Ester acted promptly and prevented what might have been an assault or robbery. Alternatively, the client might have envisioned a sexual game in which the knife would serve as a prop, but when a client already holds a knife it does not seem the best moment to find out if he is interested in playing out a 'knife-fantasy'. Leaving aside the fantasies of control and submission over a prostitute's person that some clients entertain, Ester's account stresses the high level of fear and anxiousness that daily accompany streetwalkers.

Respondents spoke of the constant danger they faced in street work and stressed that the potential of violence by clients was always present. They also called attention, however, to the fact that the bond with (some) clients constituted an emotional and/or financial resource. Or, as the women put it, some clients helped them. In time, when women realised that a third party was not there to control them constantly, they started slowly 'taking time off' from prostitution. They went home with the clients, cooked together, stayed over to watch TV, went out for dinner or to a funfair or visited the city. As these off-street activities were possible only during women's working shifts, they had to ensure that the clients paid for their time because they were required to surrender a certain amount of money per shift to the third party. It was not uncommon for clients to help out women financially, whether by giving them larger or smaller sums. At times, clients would give women a larger sum of money that covered or even exceeded the cost of time they spent together. Regular clients in particular generated a steady flow of money. For example, when Kateryna included a client in her plan to leave the street, he took it upon himself to orchestrate the financial part of it:

About 2 am, a client came and I told him: 'Look, I want to leave'. Actually, I said 'How much will you pay me for an hour?' I explained the situation a little to him and he told me 'Look, if you come with me to the hotel I'll give you 200 EUR.' I said 'Oh, OK.' I stayed for an hour. Then we spoke about how to do things since he was enthusiastic [about my plan to leave]. He was an oldie. OK, he did nothing because he couldn't, but he would still visit us to be in the company of young girls. This guy was enthusiastic and said 'Here, I have 250 EUR with me and I'll give it all to you. Later I'll give you other 250 but I need to go to the cash-machine first.' And I said 'Oh, OK'. Then he went to the cash-machine, gave me 500, bought me the train ticket and took me to the train station and there we [Kateryna and another respondent] took the train to Turin.

Some clients then helped women to improve or change their situation.[17] But it was not uncommon for clients to go through a trouble far bigger than just giving money to women. What are we to make of a client who, after being phoned by a respondent in trouble, took it upon himself to convince the third party to return the respondent's passport? Or of those clients who instructed women not to surrender all of their earnings to the third party and who kept 'safe' a part of the women's earnings or opened a bank account and deposited the woman's earnings directly? Are the clients who 'helped' the women to exit third party controlled prostitution acting out of generosity? Do they simply want to partake in women's escape 'adventures'? I suggest that for these clients the excitement did not derive so much from the commercial sexual transaction, but instead from accessing the private sphere of women's life and playing an active role in it.

This role is linked in complex ways to the issue of masculinity. Clients – male, white, Italian nationals and employed or retired – were in far more stable social and economic positions than the respondents, who were women, 'Others', undocumented, engaged in a stigmatised activity, of precarious earning and living in conditions of confinement. As studies on clients who engage with racially 'Other' prostitutes has shown, 'buying sex' from socially, politically and economically disadvantaged women who experience conditions of confinement is closely linked to Western notions of masculine honour and the capacity to harm or help others (O'Connell Davidson, 2003: 230; Nencel, 2000; Brace and O'Connell Davidson, 1996).

In their study of clients in Italy, Corso and Landi (1998: 80) asked clients if they buy sex from 'trafficked' women and one of them replied: 'Of course I do. In fact, I feel gratified afterwards because I certainly treat them better than many others [clients]. I give them a bit more money than they ask for and this way I help them'. These clients were also not simple passers-by but were habitual users of prostitutes and had previously assisted other women in similar circumstances. In fact, a number of clients who facilitated respondents' exit from prostitution later (or before) became their boyfriends but kept on buying sex from other prostitutes and assisted them in leaving prostitution too. These clients were not 'helping' an Italian woman but rather a migrant woman whom they knew was closely controlled by a third party. Moreover, they preferred women from eastern Europe: some went for women of a specific nationality, Russian for example, while others were interested in eastern European women in general. Hence, clients' preference for the respondents is closely related to women's 'Otherness' and their vulnerability due to the condition of confinement.[18] Therefore, viewing clients' 'help' simply as an act of generosity would overlook the asymmetrical power relations characteristic of the client-prostitute bond and therefore mistake power for altruism.

Leaving street prostitution

In their investigation of 'trafficked' women in Italy, Candia and Carchedi (2001: 113) found that a considerable number of women left third party controlled prostitution through their own initiatives. The authors were surprised about this finding as 'trafficking' literature has still to investigate the workings of the bond between a third party and a woman or the extent to which that bond might be open to negotiation, leading possibly to a change in a woman's contract or exit from third party controlled street prostitution. Against the emerging evidence that the largest percentage of 'trafficked' women exited exploitative situations in the sex sector unaided (Della Giusta et al., 2008: 67), it is still too often assumed that if women escape third party controlled prostitution they do so because they have been 'rescued' by their clients of the police. Little attention is paid to the relationships women establish and to the resources they themselves generate, which in turn permit them to leave the situation controlled by the third party. In the following sections, I illustrate three factors that triggered women's exit from street prostitution, namely the 'crisis moment', beliefs about femininity and material resources.

Crisis moment

Leaving street prostitution was often preceded by an episode of shock or some kind of radical change, which I refer to in terms of a 'breaking point' or a 'moment of crisis'. A way of describing this situation best is perhaps to say that we are not speaking of an everyday occurrence but rather of an exceptional event in women's lives. A number of situations offer insight into what constitutes the 'breaking point'. For Sasha, the moment of crisis was that of the trauma she experienced after a client brutally abused her best friend and peer worker, Zora. Sasha and Zora had travelled from Ukraine in order to work together in prostitution in Italy. In a quite detailed and painful rendering of that episode, Sasha spoke of a solid and important friendship that she had with Zora. Their bond was one of the major resources during that period: they supported each other emotionally and took care of each other on the street. One evening they had had a fight and so, on this occasion, Sasha did not write down the licence-plate of the client with whom Zora had left. Some time later, Zora returned on foot to the place where Sasha stood but her face was disfigured and bleeding so badly that Sasha did not recognise her, got scared, started screaming and shouted at Zora to stay away. When the police arrived, they vomited at the sight in front of their eyes. Zora was taken to a hospital and after a long period of hospitalisation, her face was readjusted through plastic surgery. After she recovered completely, she left Italy for Ukraine and broke off the friendship with Sasha. It was shortly after this traumatic incident that Sasha stopped working in street prostitution.

A similarly strong episode was experienced by Marisa, for whom the breaking point was that of the murder of a friend and peer worker with whom she had travelled to Italy. After the couple who controlled them fled Italy, Marisa and her friend remained in sex work and shared the same apartment. While Marisa managed to negotiate her own freedom from the fleeing third party, her friend got passed to another third party. Marisa's friend became involved with selling drugs and, after she incurred a large debt, she attempted to pay it off by 'stealing' women from the street and 'selling' them to third parties. After a while, Marisa's friend was found murdered and her body half burned in a park close to where Marisa worked. Since it was well known in the prostitution network that the two of them were friends, Marisa was scared that those who killed her friend might harm her too. She was also aware that the police would open an investigation and feared that they might suspect her of being involved in the murder. As a way out of this situation, Marisa opted for collaborating with the police, negotiated a residence permit and subsequently left sex work.

The death of a close friend or a family member can have 'liberatory' effects and act as the catalyst to end the situation of exploitation, as seen here in Ester's example. Ester was under strong economic pressure from home because her father was severely sick and her family needed money in order to pay for his medications. After her father died, although Ester was sad and felt guilty for not being present at the funeral, she felt relieved at the same time because the reason that bound her to a third party had now vanished:

> After [his death] I had nothing to lose; I couldn't return home because my father passed away, and I thought 'I'll try to run away'. So, I ran away. I remember when my father passed away; he died on the 30th of April, and ten days later I ran away. I did my best. [I thought] come what may. I did things slowly; it took me all these days to run away because I wasn't managing to take with me all that I had. I didn't have much but more or less I took with me all of my clothes.

Episodes of brutal physical violence, murder or death constituted 'breaking moments' that played a crucial role in women's leaving of independent or third party controlled street prostitution. Yet, however brutal or painful these moments were, they alone were not enough to set off the process that led women out of third party controlled prostitution. Other negotiations or arrangements needed to be orchestrated for an exit to take place. For Ester this meant that the decision to run away following her father's death went hand in hand with her boyfriend's promise to provide her and her sister with accommodation and money upon her leaving prostitution. The moment of crisis might have hence worked as a trigger but the possibility of leaving street prostitution was contingent on women securing financial and emotional resources.

Material Resources

In order to leave prostitution women needed to balance personal and impersonal forms of constraint. They needed to create relational or material resources that would give them at least a minimal security upon leaving prostitution. Women were very much aware that their chance of exiting third party controlled prostitution was contingent upon having alternative living arrangements and economic resources, as well as being able to obtain legal immigration status. Kateryna framed this in a clear and concise way when describing a conversation she had with clients who advised her to leave street prostitution:

> They would come and tell me: 'But you have to change; you don't feel good here.' And I would reply 'Will you help me to change? If I leave, will you help me to find a job, a house, to get documents? Will you help me to get out?' Then they would step back. I said, 'I also know the things you are telling me; why do you bother me if you know that there is nothing you can do.' I also know what is good and what is bad but it is not the same thing to know and to be able to do what one wishes for.

This excerpt shows Kateryna's awareness of her situation: in order to leave prostitution she had to arrange where to live and how to support herself.

Having and not having money influenced women's moving in and out of sex work. For some women, money was one of the resources that allowed them to leave prostitution. Marisa, Snezana and Sasha first worked for a third party and later worked on their own. Each of them had a financial goal in mind such as buying a house back home or earning a fixed sum of money to send home or to have a child. Once that goal was met, they left sex work. A number of other women left prostitution because they doubted whether the third party would pay them at all or because they did not get paid the contracted sum. For example, when the respondent who was working in street prostitution for a month was not given the payment agreed upon at the end of the month, she concluded that if she was not getting anything out of it, her project of short-term work in prostitution as a way of making money made little sense. She decided to leave but was afraid to do so alone and looked for an accomplice. She convinced another woman who had just arrived in Italy and was controlled by the same third party that staying in prostitution was a waste of time since she would never get any money from the third party. Some days later they finished their shifts, kept the money, asked a client to give them a lift to the city centre and left.

When women did not manage to secure the necessary resources on their own, they relied on clients to 'help' them out. In fact, many women established a privileged relationship with a 'habitual' client and made sure that he provided for them financially:

> If it hadn't been for that person, if I hadn't complained to him, hadn't cried on his shoulder, so to speak … I told him: 'I don't want to work on the street, I didn't come here to work on the street.' … He said: 'No, no. It shouldn't be this way that one doesn't want to work and [still] has to work. It is abnormal for people to do that.' He said: 'If you want, you can leave because, I can take you as a client.' […] In principle, he took me off the road, bought me clothes and shoes. … Of course, I couldn't show up anywhere the way I looked. … He bought me clothes and shoes and since that day. …

And since that day, that client became Maja's lover, and they engaged in a four month-long affair. He provided for her financially and bought her clothes and food. Since he was married and with children, he could not bring her home but accommodated her in a hotel where she stayed for three months. Hence, leaving street prostitution depended on women's ability to secure money and housing on their own, or to establish a relationship with clients who took it upon themselves to provide these material resources for them.

Beliefs about femininity

I would like shortly to return to the quotation in the earlier section where Maja tells of the encounter with clients who 'helped' her to exit from third party controlled prostitution and shift the terms of analysis from emphasis on material aspects of this bond to its affective dimension. When we do so, it becomes apparent that this relationship was grounded on the trust Maja felt towards the client. However, since Maja and the client hardly knew each other, the basis of this trust needs to be investigated. How did the feeling of trust emerge and gain strength? The key sentence that allows for an understanding of dynamics between Maja and the client is the following one by the client: 'No, no. It shouldn't be this way that one doesn't want to work and [still] she has to work. It is abnormal people who do that'. Whether this could mean that it is abnormal that the third party forced unwilling women into prostitution or that it is abnormal people who accept doing something against their will, the meaning remains the same. What is communicated is an acknowledgement that the respondent did not 'choose' to work on the street and therefore is not a prostitute. By phrasing it in this manner, the client disassociated Maja from sex work and confirmed her as a person rather than a 'whore'. By extension, Maja was positioned not as a participant in an 'abnormal' sphere but instead as entitled to inhabit 'normality'.

I want to suggest that women's self-representation as not-prostitutes played a crucial role in leaving prostitution, which in turn strengthened their perception of themselves as 'normal' women. In this regard, an interesting quotation comes from Liudmila, who agreed to come to Italy to work in prostitution but decided not to reveal this detail to her ex-client, now boyfriend: 'I never told him about this thing. I only told him that it is not my fault if I am working on the street; I was brought here. He also saw that I left the street; that I did not stay.' The fact that Liudmila framed leaving prostitution in these terms upheld the idea of women's migration for the sex sector in terms of deception and coercion into prostitution and of migrant women as victims of third parties. This interpretation, I suggest, was indispensable if Liudmila was to see herself as not really a prostitute. If she was to maintain her sense of self as not-prostitute she had to leave prostitution because, as she put it, she was 'working' together with 'all those shitty people there [on the street]. Good people cannot be found there, only the Moroccans and others similar to them. Ignoring for the moment the racist remark, the quote indicates that if Liudmila was to maintain self-respect and the image of herself as a special and capable person, she had to leave street prostitution because 'good' people are not to be found 'on the streets'.

It is possible to explore this dynamic further in Snezana's narrative, as it combines aspects from the both instances discussed above. She, on the one hand, let her 'habitual' client believe she was in prostitution because she was controlled by her abusive Moldavian boyfriend back home. On the other, she got confirmed as a not-prostitute through the bond with the client:

> I told him 'Massimo, I am sorry, I have a boyfriend in Moldova.' He said 'This is not for you. My love, this is not for you. He knows what are you doing here and he phones you to tell you to bring him the money.' I would have never imagined that Massimo would have told me these words. When this boyfriend of mine phoned from Moldova, Massimo changed my sim card. He told me 'This is a bad boy. Forget him. You are not made for this. I will help you.'

Massimo made the respondent his project and she let him. He instructed her how to keep a part of her earnings, he opened a bank account for her, she kept the evidence of money she sent home or saved for herself, and he told her when it was time to leave prostitution. She found an apartment in the city centre for herself, he signed the contract, she put in part of the money, and he put the rest. This arrangement created a situation of emotional and material dependency on the client, who managed both Snezana's emotional life and financial situation.

In her analysis of relationships between sex workers in the Dominican Republic and foreign male clients, Denise Brennan suggests that women entertain romantic dreams of meeting the right man who will take them to Europe but that confronted with the reality of achieving and making this dream work, women's economic imperatives outweigh a dream for a romance (Brennan, 2004). While Brennan's rather functionalist view is useful in thinking though the negotiations women put in place, my study suggests that, when considered together with women's distancing themselves from being a prostitute, the 'romance' aspect needs also to be investigated for its role in relation to women's subjectivities. The description of the bond between clients and women in terms of a 'romance' came up in several narratives. Such as, for example, when Larisa described falling in love with a 'passer-by' and leaving prostitution with words that carry a touch of romance: 'I left so suddenly ... like in Celentano's song, so suddenly'. She could leave prostitution because, as she put it, she felt the necessary inner strength to do so. As Larisa explained further, this inner strength is given only to those who are not really prostitutes. By making a distinction between 'when you are a whore inside' and 'when you are on the street', Larisa imagined herself as part of the latter category and hence able to fall in love, engage in a relationship, be welcomed at her boyfriend's house and finally leave prostitution. This establishing of a 'romantic' and 'trustworthy' relationship with a client was made possible by the absence of a commercial sexual transaction between his and Larisa: 'I trusted him because at the beginning he asked me nothing but instead gave me, we talked and he gave me money. It went on like this for more than three months'.

The absence of the 'sexual' component in Larisa's description of her romance is very similar to Ester's account of her first encounter with a client:

> I was crying on the street when I met him. I was on the sidewalk, he stopped the car, and I was drinking a Coke. He asked me something, my head was bowed, and I was crying. He stepped out of the car and asked me 'What happened? Come on, I'll do you no harm. Come on. Come for a ride'.

The encounter with this client, who in time became Ester's boyfriend and who, once Ester left the third party controlled prostitution, helped her both with money and housing, is portrayed outside the sphere of prostitution. Ester was standing on the street, with a Coke in her hand, her head low, when the client who was passing by saw her crying, stopped the car, stepped out of the car (not the usual practice when buying sex), approached her and invited her for a ride. By omitting explicit reference to the situation of prostitution and locating the encounter outside the realm of sexual work, Ester's framing of the episode gives an image of a romantic encounter. Ester's description of her first encounter with her future boyfriend is quite similar to that of yet another respondent, Oksana. Shortly before Oksana met her current partner, she split her evening meal – a sandwich – with her best friend Ioanna. With half a sandwich in hand she was standing on the street when a car stopped and she got in. As Oksana put it, as soon as she and the client looked into each others' eyes, she felt an immediate feeling of trust and offered him half of her half-sandwich. These accounts romanticise the encounter, in particular when referring to trust and instinct, and move it outside the sphere of prostitution and into a romantic relationship among 'equal' partners, as Oksana's offer of her half-sandwich symbolically conveys.

Studies of non-migrant prostitution interpret women's distancing themselves from being a prostitute in terms of a 'coping strategy' and a way in which women separated their private from their working selves (O'Neill and Berberet, 2000; O'Neill, 2001; McKeganey and Barnard, 1996). Moreover, scholars have shown that women in sex work differentiate between a whore and a non-whore as a way of rejecting social identification as a prostitute. For this separation to work, women need to be acknowledged as such within a heterosexual 'romantic' relationship (Nencel, 2000). Given the fact that this separation is premised on downplaying the commercial basis of a sexual transaction in sex work, I put forward the suggestion that this dynamic constituted an important incentive for leaving sex work and for the construction of migrant woman's subjectivities. I take up and explore in detail the issue of disavowal of prostitution and constitution of subjectivities in the Chapter 4.

Conclusion

A differentiation between personal and impersonal forces allowed for a detailed analysis of what constitutes the conditions of confinement and how these are maintained. Such an unfolding of women's working lives permitted the identification of a set of resources that women generated in order to gain mobility and mitigate the conditions of confinement. The variety of relationships women established and the resources women engendered enabled them to exit third party controlled prostitution and work independently, or to exit street work all together. Concepts such as 'sexual slavery' are not adequate to understand women's lives in third party controlled prostitution as they conceal the complexity and interdependence of various factors that constitute the condition of confinement as well as the degree of agency women exercise despite exploitative labour conditions and various forms of abuse that accompany street prostitution. Police or clients' active intervention are thus not indispensable preconditions if women are to exit third party controlled street prostitution. Seemingly insignificant factors, such as women's beliefs about femininity can also trigger the decision to leave prostitution.

4
Multiple Scripts: Mothers, Whores and Victims

'A whore! I fear this word.'
Ivana

Introduction

In Chapters 2 and 3, my discussion of women's projects of migration and the factors that triggered exit from street prostitution touched upon the importance of gender for our analysis. In Chapter 2, I suggested that women's migration could be read in terms of an escape route from oppressive patriarchal structures and in particular from situations of intra-family violence. Interestingly, respondents systematically glossed over these episodes of violence and did not include or expand on family abuse in the interviews; however, I got to know of these through informal conversations. The omissions of episodes of violence permitted the women to take up the position of protagonists in their narrative of migration, which might have been undermined by description of endured violence. Moreover, whereas women spoke of poverty as the main reason for migrating abroad, the recurring reference to poverty, in particular consistently at the very opening of the interviews, prompted me to pay close attention to the function that this reference plays in women's narratives. I suggested that what I called the 'motif of poverty' performs a narrative function of enabling respondents to contrast poverty with prostitution and to distance themselves from being identified as prostitutes. This act of distancing is achieved, as I illustrated in Chapter 3, by downplaying the commercial transaction in sex work and framing it instead in terms of a romantic encounter. I suggested further that this permitted migrant women to sustain the construct of themselves as not really prostitutes and that this offers important insights into women's subjectivities.

I develop these considerations further in this chapter and focus on the tensions and contradictions in the women's narratives. I ask why and how did those very same women who, when it came to their histories of family abuse, emphasised their active role in carrying out their migration projects, come to downplay these efforts when the discussion turned to their involvement in sex work. In order to make sense of this dynamic, I pay attention to the legal dimension of immigration regulations as well as to the norms and values around femininity. These are examined both in relation to Italy as the country of migration as well as in the women's communities of origin. The structural location that respondents inhabited in Italy is best described as that of social and legal marginality.

Contrary to respondents' expectations of social, economic and affective mobility, in Italy they experienced a situation of constraint and confinement to street prostitution. Imposed by third parties and enforced by restrictive immigration regulations, this situation reduced migrant women's spatial and labour mobility. If upon exiting street prostitution migrant women significantly increased their mobility they nevertheless remained confined spatially, socially and labour-wise due to their immigrant status and the moral stigma surrounding prostitution. The divergent positions that women occupy, and constantly negotiate, are considered in relation to illegality and stigmatisation in as much as legal schemes and gender and sexuality norms result in women either gaining rights under the VoT protection scheme or, if identified as prostitutes, deportation and further marginalisation by their communities of origin.

To make visible women's efforts to negotiate and remain loyal to a set of social positions such as those of migrant, victim, mother, wife and sex worker that are not compatible with the discursive and legal schemes pertaining to sex trafficking, is to pay attention to the formation of women's subjectivities and the importance of gender difference in relation to the constitution of the subject. Studies about 'trafficked' women disagree about how to best define this category of women: should they be seen as victims of crime, both when it comes to non-consensual migration and labour exploitation? Or should they be seen instead as labour migrants and therefore as migrant sex workers who entered sex work consensually? These positions draw an unfeasible distinction between 'victims' and 'agents' and presuppose a static notion of the subject.

Women's subjectivities, I suggest in this chapter, are constituted through migration and prostitution and do not map neatly onto any one of the categories. Even when they overlap with those categories, as in the case of women identifying as victims, the narrative of victim-hood is not solely imposed upon women but rather needs to be examined for the appeal it holds for stigmatised migrant subjects who pursue social and legal inclusion. In what follows, I discuss how respondents dealt with the impact of objectification and stigma during and after the time they spent in street prostitution. I examine practices and discourses via which migrant women struggled to avoid marginalisation both in Italy and in their communities of origin. I pay attention in particular to the role of the silence and of the mother-daughter relationships in maintaining of gender and sexuality boundaries in women's countries of origins. In Italy, I show that the relationship women had with Italian men and the granting of the residence permit for VoTs played a very similar role in downplaying stigmatisation and facilitating migrant women's social acceptance. In the final part of this chapter, I turn to examining how norms around gender and sexuality informed respondents' investments in the migratory project and how these determined the multiple social positions that women took up and through which they negotiated various contradictions produced by the discursive and juridical regimes that regulate their lives.

The whore stigma

The respondents invariably set off from their counties of origin in order to create new opportunities for themselves and to achieve social mobility. Upon their arrival in Italy and confinement within third party controlled street prostitution, they were faced, however, with a situation of immobility. Not only were they spatially confined but they were also faced with specific forms of confinement caused by their work in prostitution. In addition to the limits the third parties imposed on respondents' movement, inhabiting the 'space' of prostitution meant being exposed to objectification and stigmatisation. The fear of stigmatisation, due to their work in the sex industry, accompanied the respondents also after they had exited prostitution.

Objectification and the fear of lasting stigmatisation

For the clients, the attraction of commercial sex often lies in the limited and unemotional nature of contact, the absence of commitment and the possibility to evade obligations and responsibilities towards the prostitute (O'Neill, 2001; Corso and Landi, 1998; O'Connell Davidson, 1998: 134; McKeganey and Barnard, 1996: 52). The uneasiness and pain involved in being viewed as a sexualised object instead of a subject with her own history and needs was addressed by the respondents in several accounts. Ester described various episodes in which, when in a car with a client (and at times his wife too) and feeling miserable, crying and asking for his help, he would pretend not to hear her and continue to demand the sexual service. Marisa noted that when one is seen as a whore, men treat you without respect, and don't include you in their everyday life and social networks: 'You cannot talk or go out with anyone without being treated as a whore. He does not take you seriously. He speaks to you as to a whore. Then, he goes home and you stay alone'. When reflecting on her experience of street work, Kateryna paralleled the accounts of another two respondents when she differentiated between being perceived by men as a prostitute and therefore as a sexualised object and as a person whose subjectivity is recognised and acknowledged:

> When you're on the street, you're there and the one who looks at you knows that he can fuck you if he has the money. When the clients arrive they look at you as an object: move here, move there. They don't look at you as a woman with her character and her personality. One looks at you exactly as an object, a doll; if he wants you, he takes you. He doesn't ask you what do you think, doesn't want to know your opinion about something, won't start debating politics with you. But when he looks at you from the other angle meaning as a person, as a character, and he sees the things you want and don't want, then it is different because he sees you differently knowing what you have done, meaning who you have been. It's more difficult to have a relationship, even a non sexual one, when he sees you as a person with your problems.

In rendering the difference between a commercial sexual contact and a non-commercial bond, Kateryna articulated that objectification entailed the operation, enhanced by the position of clients' (economic) power, of reducing ones' complexities to that of a controllable sexualised object.[1] This sexualised objectification went hand in hand with moral stigmatisation. The 'whore stigma' establishes a differentiation between decent and indecent, chaste and unchaste, worthy and unworthy women (Scambler and Scambler, 1997; Pheterson, 1996). In this symbolic organisation, the latter attributes become the Other of 'proper' femininity and are associated with the prostitute. The 'whore stigma' demarcates the separation between 'deviant' and 'normal' femininity and carries a large range of legal and social consequences for those characterised as 'whores'. The fear of the 'whore stigma' and of its consequences permeates women's narratives. This is best visible from the fact that most respondents decided not to disclose their involvement in sex work to their friends, family and partners. Those who met their partners while in prostitution, and continued a relationship with them after ceasing to do sex work, preferred not to discuss the matter further. Among the respondents there is only one, Kateryna, who spoke of sex work migration with her partner in an explicit manner:

> To have a relationship with a man without telling him about my past and letting him know me only as I am today, even though he might feel gratified exactly because he does not know, would however mean for me keeping this relationship unsatisfactory.

For Kateryna, countering the 'whore stigma' implied exposing both her strengths and weaknesses to her partner. This openness about her work in prostitution was seen as a necessary condition for her relationship to gain in strength and develop. Kateryna, who legalised her immigration status after several years of living in Italy, found accommodation in a shared flat, found a job and established a long-term relationship with an ex-client of hers, thereby attaining a certain amount of stability. In contrast, most of the respondents, who were in much more precarious legal, working and living situations, preferred not to discuss the matter of sex work migration with their partners. When speaking of prostitution to their partners, they were ambiguous about the terms of the labour 'contract' they entered with third parties or maintained that they have been coerced into migration and sex work. Liudmila offers an example: 'I never told him about it. I simply told him that it's not my fault that I am here. ... [I told him] I was brought here. I told him things this way and according to me, I did the right choice.' In this quotation, Liudmila emphasises that not telling her Italian partner (ex-client) that she could migrate to Italy only on the condition of working in prostitution, was 'the right choice'. By framing it in this manner, Liudmila expresses the fear that her partner would not understand her reasons and, instead of seeing her as someone who ended up in prostitution forcefully, would perceive her as a woman who has 'chosen' prostitution of her own accord and perceive her thus as a 'whore'.

Another respondent discussed the consequences of such a classification. In an imaginary conversation between a woman who was involved in sex work and a man she was engaged with, Maja speculated about how a man would react if a woman was to tell him about prostitution: 'If she told him [about prostitution], he might say, "I don't need you like this.

I can find another one who didn't work on the road"'. The stigmatisation and social condemnation were almost always seen by the respondents as seriously endangering their chances of having a 'serious' relationship or getting married. The respondents feared the consequences of the 'whore stigma' that classifies women as either 'innocent' women or 'guilty whores'. Ana addressed the matter in the following manner:

> There are people in Italy and everywhere else that say 'You whore'. They want to be with you for a while in order to fuck you and then they leave. Even if they like me they will not marry me because the marriage is something else, something more. See, I say to myself, 'OK. Things [arrival in Italy and prostitution] went this way when I was 20 years old, but I want to live. It is not my fault, I am young and never in my life did I harm someone or do something bad to a person'.

Ana criticised the moral stigma attached to prostitution as well as the fact that those women who are labelled 'whores' lose the respect and social status men accord to non-prostitutes. Moreover, she disapproved of the social representations of prostitution, which characterise women as delinquents and result in lasting stigma.

The stigma does not affect women's lives only while in prostitution but accompanies them long afterwards and can be brought up at any stage later in their lives. For this very reason, those women who established relationships with Italian men (not ex-clients) after having left prostitution, preferred not to disclose this part of their lives to their boyfriends. The fear of possible stigmatisation emerged in a recollection of a conversation between one respondent and her new boyfriend, whom she met in a factory where they both worked. On one occasion, the respondent asked her boyfriend if he knew those women on the streets. After he told Marisa of being a client himself, she asked him:

> 'Excuse me, you were together with that girl and if you liked it, why did you not go with her the second time? Can you not fall in love with her?' He tells me 'Not even once have I thought of staying together with a person who works on the street. Even if I would meet her somewhere else and she tells me she has worked on the street, I would feel bitterness. She is not a person I am looking for.'

In this conversation, whether imaginary or real, we see the respondent's own situation, her fear of stigmatisation and objectification, and of the consequent negation of the position she has so far acquired in Italian society. The fear of stigma and social condemnation therefore characterised women's lives also after having left sex work. During a group discussion, the women were unanimous in agreeing that it was irrelevant how long one had worked in prostitution; the stigma arose from having worked on the street full stop, and one could be reproached at any time later in life.

Next to fearing stigmatisation from their partners, women feared public disclosure and stigmatisation too. It is not uncommon for a woman that is blond and presumed to be Russian to be suspected of being a prostitute and harassed verbally or physically. In some countries such as Turkey, Israel, England and the US, the name Natasha has become a synonym for a prostitute and is used as a common denigrating label for all women from the eastern European region, whether they are sex workers or not. While Gülçür and İlkkaracan (2002) do not include Italy in their list of countries where the term Natasha has gained discursive currency, women's accounts of their daily life in Bologna show that, whether due to one's physical appearance or a way of dressing, they too have been affected by the discourse that conflates women from former Russian states with prostitutes. Snezana mentioned a public gathering on Bologna's central square where a priest, Don Benzi, gave a speech on trafficking and where women he 'saved' from prostitution delivered testimonies. While listening to the women's stories, a man from the audience standing next to Snezana looked at her and grabbed her by her arm. He then told her that it was her turn to give a testimony as he could tell that she was not Italian and had worked in prostitution.

In order to avoid such exposure, some respondents did not speak in their mother tongues when in public and used Italian instead. Some broke contacts with other women with whom they had previously worked on the street and who also remained in Italy upon leaving sex work. Others were extremely careful about the way they dressed, especially since the dress code in its intersection with being a migrant woman sufficed to label one as a prostitute. Sasha stopped wearing short skirts in order not to attract people's attention and to avoid potential stigmatisation:

> You know, when I go to work I dress normally. If you dress in a skirt or something similar they look at you immediately. The Italians are like this. If you know that it is like this, that you are a foreigner and that they can look at you, then please – for your own good – dress differently. Try to dress in a way so they do not look at you immediately. Once Oksana was here and Mauro [a friend] was waiting outside for

me. Oksana was going to work at the grandmother's of whom she was taking care. He does not know Oksana and he tells me 'Do you see this blond [girl] over there? One can see that she is a whore.' It was he who told me this.

Sasha, who had left street work several years ago and who, at the time of the interview, had an employment contract as a cleaner, voiced her fear of being recognised as a foreigner and by association as a (former) prostitute. Whether this conversation took place in exactly this form or not is of no real importance for the current investigation. What is important is that through an Italian male, the respondent communicated the impact on her of the existing identification of women from former Russia with prostitutes. The fact that an Italian man articulated the words further validated Sasha's anxiety about societal refusal and displayed her awareness of how power relations operate and whose words count in conferring social acceptance. Since objectification and the fear of stigmatisation impacted women's lives both during and after leaving sex work, they were constantly confronted with and had to balance the fact that being labelled a 'whore' would confine them to the narrow designation of 'the prostitute' and jeopardise their migratory projects by undermining their precarious social acceptance.

Countries of origin: Pushing against boundaries of gender and sexuality

Having worked in prostitution for a shorter or a longer period of time implied a recurring threat of stigmatisation in particular if women's work in prostitution became public knowledge. Whether they stayed in Italy or returned to their countries of origin, respondents inevitably had to negotiate the gender and sexuality norms within these communities. In what follows, I discuss the importance of silence, which I refer to in terms of a 'tacit agreement', and the role of the mother–daughter relationship in maintaining gender and sexuality boundaries in women's communities of origin.

Silence as a tacit agreement

In her analysis of the relationship between imaginary communities and prostitution, Julia O'Connell Davidson highlights the political dimension of sexuality and its investment in the creation and maintenance of communities and in safeguarding the hierarchies within those communities along the lines of class, race, gender, age and social status.

Those who break these boundaries (such as prostitutes) are excluded from enjoying full citizen's rights, become 'outsiders' and are prevented from returning to their communities (O'Connell Davidson, 1998). Building on the discussion of community and its boundaries, my data show that it is possible for women who have worked in the sex sector to remain part of a given community on condition that their involvement in prostitution is kept secret. By secret I mean a tacit agreement between members of a community not to acknowledge prostitution explicitly. The majority of those respondents who returned home, as well as those who stayed in Italy, decided not to tell their families of their work in prostitution. Sasha, for example, explained that in her hometown in Ukraine, a vast number of young women migrated abroad to work in prostitution. This fact is known within her community but, as she put it, 'no one talks about it and it is better that way'. So, even though women's migration for labour in the sex industry has been occurring in the countries of eastern Europe and fSU for about a decade, and some of the respondents have travelled in and out of their communities in order to work in the sex industry or knew of other women who did this, migrant women, their families and communities all maintain a silence with regard to sex work migration.

In order to understand this better, let me give an example. Imagine a small city where for over a decade a large population of young women has travelled abroad to work in prostitution. Some of them have sent money back and others returned home. Those who brought money home presented their earnings in cash and usually accompanied it with presents for all. Someone's return from a foreign country is often a cause for celebration for the whole family. Extended families come together and celebrate the woman who has just returned. Her family is proud of her and she is seen as a model for other young people in that family or community. If it were made explicit that the money had been earned through prostitution, the admiration would give place to shame. For this very reason, respondents preferred to search for solutions that would enable them to carry on their migratory projects on their own terms rather than being returned home through an NGO or a programme assisting VoTs. Being deported, especially as a result of a police roundup, would mean returning home unannounced and usually without any money. If a woman managed to put aside some money or deposit it in a bank, a deportation would mean that she was unable to access that money. Similarly, given the fact that the contracts between third parties and the women were usually for a three-month period, being deported ahead of time meant not being paid at all, suffering an economic loss and being perceived as a failed migrant upon returning home. Stigmatisation hence occurs as a consequence of the social norms attached to both prostitution as well as failed migration usually associated with being deported or returning home without money. Prostitution *and* failed migration, as a study of VoTs in eastern Europe has shown, are not separate but rather mutually reinforce each other in producing stigmatisation (Brunovskis and Surtees, 2007: 128).

The tacit agreement of silence between women, their families and other community members put the respondents in a precarious position. An example comes from Larisa who, after she reached Italy, prostituted first under the control of an Albanian man and later negotiated a contract for sex work with a female friend of hers. When Larisa went to the police to press charges against the Albanian third party, her female friend was scared that the respondent would press charges against her too and left Italy to return to her (and Larisa's) hometown in Moldova. She then made public that Larisa had worked as a prostitute in Italy. The respondent interpreted this as a consequence of the woman's fear that her unexpected return after many years in Italy would be seen as related to prostitution. Hence, in order to remove all doubt she offloaded the potential stigma onto the respondent. For Larisa, having been publicly denounced as a prostitute meant deciding to stay in Italy as she considered it impossible to return to her home community because, as she put it, 'her reputation had been ruined'. Larisa regarded being exposed as a prostitute as an offence of such magnitude that, in order to redress the damage, she decided to press charges against her female friend. This friend, along with her husband, was consequently charged with exploitation of prostitution.

On those rare occasions that a respondent decided to make explicit that she had worked in prostitution, she did so by telling the family member closest to her and relying on him/her not to tell others. Ivana, who decided to return home to Croatia after exiting third party controlled prostitution and pressing charges against the third party, told her husband that she had worked in prostitution. However, she decided not to tell him how many clients she had during those 20 days. She told him she saw five clients, omitting approximately other 390. This decision was informed by Ivana's fear that her husband would refuse her once he knew the real number. She was afraid that he would be disgusted by her and would not want to touch her any longer because, as she puts it, she might have been 'contaminated'. Once she told her husband about her work in street prostitution, they decided together not to say anything about it to any other family members since they both feared the consequences of such a disclosure. They thought that his father would surely force them to divorce and call her a whore. At the same time, Ivana was convinced that her own father would also call her a whore, accuse her of being just like her mother who was 'unfaithful' to him, and conclude that the mother deserved all the beatings he gave her. Hence, making prostitution explicit even to the person closest to the respondent entailed simultaneously negotiating one's own position in relation to her husband and their common position as a couple towards a larger social setting. In both instances, women feared the rejection and punishment reserved for those whose behaviour deviates from societal gender and sexual norms.

Among those respondents who stayed in Italy, it was highly uncommon to reveal their work in prostitution to a family member in their country of origin. Geographical distance, photos of Italy's most known tourist sites, remittances and short visits home accompanied by presents for the whole family all made it possible to avoid suspicion about the type of work the women did in Italy. My study offers one exception to this rule and shows under what conditions it was possible for a woman to disclose information about her work in the sex sector. To summarise briefly, Kateryna accepted her male lover's proposal to come to Italy and work in prostitution. This decision was informed by her passionate and desperate desire to change her life, namely improve her economic situation, relieve her depression and achieve emotional autonomy from her mother. After having spent five months in third party-controlled street prostitution and earning little money, Kateryna decided to leave prostitution and attempt to search for opportunities elsewhere. The exit was followed by a period in which the respondent created her resources anew: she obtained a residence and work permit for VoTs, got a job as an apprentice hairdresser, and found a room in a shared flat. During the year in Italy, she told her mother that she worked in prostitution. Her breaking of her silence around prostitution was also parallel to a shift in roles that occurred between Kateryna and her mother. Kateryna, having regained control over her life and her self-esteem, was now the one financially providing for the mother, who was by now divorced and without income. The economic and emotional stability Kateryna gained endowed her with new authority. She was now the one who earned money and performed the caring role. In her words, 'I need to look after her and take care of things'. This reversal of authority in the mother-daughter relationship, economic security and emotional stability, along with settling in Italy and the weakening of connections to the community of origin, made it all possible for Kateryna to break the silence surrounding sex work and discuss it openly with her mother. Yet, as a rule and confirming the findings of other studies of both migrant and non-migrant prostitution in various countries, in order to avoid stigmatisation and marginalisation women for the most part do not to speak of their work in prostitution to their families or network of acquaintances (Brennan, 2004; Nencel, 2000; Skrobanek et al., 1997).

Mother-daughter relationships

Mother-daughter relationship played a key role in sustaining the silence that permitted migrant women's acceptance in their communities of origin. Respondents did not disclose to their mothers that they worked in the sex sector in Italy. Kateryna's account is, as I mentioned above, an exception. Other women considered bringing up the topic with their mothers but decided against it. The rationale behind this decision was not to make their mothers worry or be hurt. Not speaking of prostitution was certainly based on women's concern for their mothers but also on their own feeling of shame and fear of their family's rejection. Marisa put it this way:

> When I went back home, I was ashamed to say anything. All the time I was lying to my mother. I didn't tell her that I was there [on the street]. If I'd told her that I've worked on the street, she'd have felt really bad. She raised me differently. It's better if no one knows. ... I don't have the courage and I don't want, I don't want to tell. I'd feel bad. They [the parents] would feel bad. For them, I would be a whore and not a daughter with a strong family as I am now. It is better it stays a secret of mine, without telling it to anyone else.

Marisa, from her position as a daughter, pointed to the pain that the knowledge of prostitution would cause her mother. She further remarked that the disclosure of her working in the sex sector would make her lose her self-respect, her position as a 'good' daughter and the image of belonging to a functional and strong family.

Marisa saying 'She raised me differently' re-echoes other respondents' words of why they found it impossible to talk of prostitution with their mothers. Ester, for her part, tried to imagine her mother finding out that her two daughters worked in prostitution in Italy and concluded that their mother would see it as an inadequacy to provide emotionally and materially for her daughters and hence as a sign of her failure as a mother.

Another respondent put herself in the place of her mother and described the negative impact she thought the disclosure of sex work might have:

> I could never tell this to my mother because I am scared she would shout at me, hate me, kick me out of the house. Later she would feel bad because the things went the way they went, because I have worked on the street, made this money, bought this furniture. ... No, I never though of telling her because she would feel really, really bad. She would start thinking that she as a mother could not offer me anything and that this is why I left and found this money, this job.

The importance of the mother-daughter relationship is therefore not to be underestimated as it points to the fact that the overseeing of sexual codes and gendered boundaries of the communities was left for the women to maintain. When their work in prostitution got publicly denounced, some women thought that 'disappearing' until the situation got calmer was the best solution.[2] Others, like Larisa, saw lying about their migratory project and stressing that they were coerced into prostitution as the best option. Silence about prostitution is what permitted women to return to their home communities and allowed the communities to maintain the appearance of unaltered gender and sexual arrangements. One of earlier studies on 'trafficking' showed that once the researchers raised the issue of prostitution with women's communities of origin and made known that women from the community worked in prostitution abroad, various people, in particular the women's mothers, were angry about this disclosure. The resulting stigmatisation compelled women to remain silent about their experiences abroad or leave and live elsewhere (Skrobanek et al., 1997: 82).

If suspected of prostitution, women might even get pressured by their mothers to migrate again. One reason for this reaction is the fear that the stigma might affect also the woman's family or community. Silence surrounding sex work migration certainly fosters misinformation about the working and living conditions migrant women encounter abroad. Yet it seems important to note that this dynamic allows women to contravene communities' gender and sexual boundaries and still return to those communities without being labelled as outcasts. The tacit agreement of silence permits women's families to enjoy the remittances and improve their social standing through having a family member abroad who succeeded in her migratory project. While I believe it is crucial to give women the tools to migrate safely, it seems to me it is also important to consider the possible drawbacks of anti-trafficking campaigns in women's countries of origin and of the assistance programmes designed to 'reintegrate' women into their communities as these contravene community's unspoken rule of keeping silent about sex work migration.

Relationships with men as inclusion strategies

Having achieved a certain degree of mobility upon leaving third party controlled prostitution, those migrant women who opted to stay in Italy needed to contend first with stigmatisation surrounding prostitution and prejudice towards women from eastern Europe and Russia, and second with being undocumented and therefore vulnerable to arrest and deportation. In the following section I discuss two key venues that women made use of and the concessions they made in order to achieve social and legal recognition. These are a relationship to an Italian boyfriend and the residence permit for VoTs.

Boyfriends and social venues of inclusion

If in their communities of origin, women's work in prostitution was managed through a tacit agreement of silence, while in Italy, sex work was occasionally acknowledged in their relationships with the Italian boyfriends. This was the case mainly in the relationships that immediately followed the women's exit from prostitution. It needs to be kept in mind that some women entered into these relationships while working on the street and were assisted by the boyfriends in leaving prostitution. In this case, it was not uncommon for the respondent to get introduced to the boyfriend's family and for the latter to know of women's past work in prostitution. Others met their boyfriends through former clients at a later stage after having already left prostitution. This constituted a crucial difference between the women's communities of origin and their relationships in Italy. The fact that respondents dated Italian men who were acquainted with their past work in prostitution allowed some space for them to include sex work as part of their accounts of migration.

These relationships were nevertheless precarious as women remained vulnerable to stigmatisation, which they tried to counteract by upholding the story of being deceived into migrating to Italy or by investing in the romantic image of love. From the emphasis that the women placed on the importance of marriage or the 'romantic' aspect of their relationship with an Italian boyfriends, it might appear that they were eager to get married or were engaged in blissfully romantic relationships. When asked specifically whether they would marry their boyfriends or if they were in love with them, respondents' answers offered a quite different picture. Marisa, for example, who beamed with happiness after each date with her new boyfriend and who spoke of them getting closer and closer to getting married, was still wary when asked specifically if she would marry him:

> For me marriage already happened once. I don't want to do it a second time ... in order to marry I've got to think through it really well. We can live together for a while without being married. We can do many things without marrying. For now, I don't want to marry.

Hence, Marisa did not exclude marriage but neither did she embrace it in an easy and unproblematic way. On the contrary, she stated that she prefers to look for arrangements alternative to marriage.

Similarly, the depiction of the relationship with an Italian boyfriend as a 'romance' did not match women's answers to the question of whether they were in love with the boyfriends. Women said that they were not in love with their boyfriends but that they were together with them out of habit. Thus, although women portrayed their first encounters with their boyfriends in a romanticised manner, they spoke of their relationships in much more sober terms. The common term used by women to describe their feeling towards the boyfriends was to say that they were fond of them. Ester, for example, phrased it in the following way:

> I'm fond of him [and] I'm fine with it. Now I'm used to him because when I go somewhere I don't pay attention to other men at all ... Listen, I don't think I'll find someone better than him. I won't send to hell a person who cares about me! [He'd tell me] 'Who do you think you are!? I took you from the street and you treat me like this?!' We don't fight; we are calm.

When reflecting upon their current relationships, women were very much aware of the affective limits of their relationships. They weighed up the intensity of their emotional investment against feelings of being cared for and accepted emotionally and socially. Women's narratives show their awareness of the disparity between the romanticised relationship or marriage and the more realistic considerations of these arrangements. However, if we do not prioritise this apparent contradiction but rather pay attention to what is attained by both desiring and dismissing marriage as an option and by inciting romance while accepting it as unrealistic, then it becomes clear that both situations allow women to create distance from being prostitutes. From this perspective, the relationship with an Italian boyfriend functions as a vehicle of societal acceptance usually denied to prostitutes. Given the stakes for women, it is of little surprise that the men's nationality mattered a great deal. This is best visible in Oksana's description of whom she would and would not date:

> I would never be together with an Albanian: I don't like their kind. With a black man, no way! Yugoslav men are all pimps or thieves. Russians, no: I don't want to because our men think only of vodka and spending money. I don't know any Americans but I could give it a thought. But now I am in Italy and therefore I am together with Italians.

Oksana's view is certainly very pragmatic ('I am in Italy and therefore I am together with Italians') but the classification she sets up is worth considering closely as it establishes a very clear hierarchy of masculinity on the basis of nationality. As we see, not all of the intersections of nationality and masculinity are given the same value: men from a national background or from communities positioned as 'Other' within Italian society are looked down upon and depicted as unsuitable, while others (such as Italians or Americans) are identified as desirable. This hierarchical ordering of masculinities on the basis of an economic and nationality scale exemplifies the importance women ascribed to the relationship with Italian men. It enabled them to achieve a certain degree of financial security due to these men's financial resources and avoid the social marginalisation and stigmatisation reserved for migrant prostitutes.

That Italian men played a crucial role in the women's lives when it comes to avoiding social and economic marginalisation is best visible in Sasha's account of giving birth. Sasha had already been in Italy for three years at the time of the interview and described her choice to remain in Italy as a succession of obstacles. The largest occurred while in a hospital in Bologna, about to give birth. Let me shortly recapitulate the events that brought Sasha there: after she left prostitution, Sasha had a relationship with an ex-client, got pregnant and decided to have a child. When her boyfriend heard about the pregnancy he said he was not ready to become a father and left. In order to provide for the child, Sasha went back to prostitution and worked independently for a number of months until she earned enough money to provide for herself and the child, and then left street prostitution again. After having given birth and while still in the hospital, she realised that the social worker wanted to take her child away. The doctors and social workers asked her whether she had money to support herself and the child, how she earned that money and what she would do when she ran out of money. She told them she would go home and take the child with her. While commenting on the behaviour of doctors and social workers, Sasha concluded that she was treated this way because she was an illegal foreigner suspected of being a prostitute. She concluded that if she was to keep her child, she needed to prove that she had a place to live and a lot of Italian friends. Sasha stressed this latter point twice: 'That's what is important. Your friends must be Italian. If they are foreigners, it's of no use.' She asked all of her male friends to come and visit her and to bring other Italian friends along. Some of them arrived with their mothers. Sasha said that this was of crucial importance because then the doctors could see her in the company of older Italian women and hear them speak Italian. The way Sasha handled the matter clearly reflected her understanding of the precarious position migrant women working in the sex sector occupy in Italian society. Her struggle to keep her child was won by having sufficient financial resources, mastering the Italian language, and displaying her 'integration' within Italian society by means of significant social bonds. It was no coincidence that Sasha did not invite any of her Russian, Moldovan or Ukrainian female friends with whom she worked in street prostitution to the hospital. For Sasha, as for other women who stayed in Italy, their relationships with Italian men countered the moral stigma reserved for prostitutes and mitigated the situation of illegality and, as such, constituted a crucial vehicle for women seeing themselves as not really prostitutes and for avoiding social ostracism.

Residence permit and legal venues of 'inclusion'

Relationships with Italian men were crucial but not the only avenue of inclusion for migrant women. Legal avenues of inclusion, such as a resident permit devised specifically for VoTs, played an equally important role in permitting the women's social and legal acceptance. Italy has a unique clause, Article 18 of its Immigration Law 40, that provides a six-month residence and work permit to foreign nationals in order to escape/exit the conditions of violence imposed by criminal organisations and to take part in the programme of social integration. Initially formulated especially for women trafficked to the sex industry but applying to all migrants in situations of abuse or severe exploitation by criminal organisations, the permit for VoTs is granted on the condition that the applicant leaves prostitution and joins a programme of social assistance and reintegration run by various community projects and NGOs. The specificity and uniqueness of the Italian provision is that granting of the permit is legally not tied to a person's willingness to take part in legal proceeding against the third parties. However, as the experience of various NGOs has shown, on the ground it is quite exceptional to be granted the VoT status without having pressed charges and testified against a third party (Pearson, 2002: 144).

The importance of such a provision cannot be underestimated and it constituted an extremely important factor in enabling women to exit situations of abuse and achieve a legal status in Italy, empowering them therefore on two crucial fronts. At the same time, however, programmes designed to assist 'victims of sex trafficking' establish a normative narrative of victimhood whereby women are seen as passive and powerless victims (Crowhurst, 2007). Article 18 sutures 'trafficking' to particular forms and patterns of violence and penalises those women whose situation fall out of the established norm. Oksana explained that when pressing charges against the traffickers in order to qualify for the permit for VoTs, she needed to include a statement that falsely affirmed that a return home to Ukraine would constitute a risk for her safety due to the threats she received from the third party. When the threat of violence on returning home or the danger of retaliation was not clearly discernible from a woman's story, immigration officers did not accept her claim to stay in Italy. Sasha's request for a residence permit on the basis of Article 18 was rejected and justified as follows: 'Currently, there are no concrete dangers for the safety of the claimant, which would be caused by the claimant's attempt to escape organisations that exploit prostitution'. Presenting oneself as a victim is therefore indispensable if a woman is to avoid deportation and attain the residence permit for VoTs.[3]

Associating violence with victims leads to the situation whereby some of the institutions providing assistance to women opted for keeping women within locked structures so as to protect them from a third party's retaliations. This situation, often combined with the attempt to 're-educate' the women away from 'vice' or 'sin', produced situations that women did not tolerate and from which they ran away. Accounts of three respondents who ran away from three different religious shelters illustrate this point best. After having left prostitution Ana, Liudmila and Oksana were housed and assisted for a brief period by various religious institutions. Oksana and Liudmila stayed a couple of days and then left because of the strictly imposed discipline, social isolation due to the countryside location, prohibition to go to the city centre and bans on smoking and on seeing their boyfriends. People 'there are idle and time disappears', said Ana, who explained that she had to leave the shelter since staying there would have meant wasting her time doing nothing. 'Only losers stay there', commented Liudmila, while describing how she secretly arranged to have her boyfriend pick her up in front of the shelter and drive her away. The conditions imposed upon women by Catholic institutions that aimed to 'assist' them therefore imposed immobility and thereby clashed with women's projects to achieve economic, social and affective mobility through migration. Imposed social isolation, discipline and surveillance impinge on women's autonomy and paradoxically resemble the situation of control these women endured while working in third party-controlled prostitution (Brunovskis and Surtees, 2007; Maluccelli, 2001: 78).

While my results confirm that the type of assistance shelters provided stood in the way of respondents realising their migratory projects, I would like to put forward the idea that women's rejection of certain types of assistance would gain in understanding if thought of in relation to issues of femininity and sexuality. As I discussed earlier, it was not uncommon for women to take up the position of a victim towards the authorities or their boyfriends in order to counter stigmatisation or legalise their immigration status. Crucially, this in turn allowed them to create distance from the social position of a prostitute. Marisa, for example, told that being granted a residence permit made her feel 'very clean in her heart'. In fact, when discussing why some of their acquaintances were not granted the Article 18 residence permits, the respondents did not question the immigration procedures but rather considered that other women did not receive permits because, as one respondent put it, they did not deserve the permit by which she implied that other women were whores.

And yet, despite the fact that the assistance provided by the religious shelters could provide women with an avenue for legalisation and counter stigmatisation, women nevertheless refused to be assisted by the shelters and ran away. Why is this so? It appears that the rules such as early wake-up calls, plain food, simple dress, daily prayers and smoking and sex bans were not only aimed at disciplining women's behaviour but also at suppressing women's sexuality. As such they were met with hostility by respondents who escaped to be with their boyfriends or to return to sex work. A quote from the feminist philosopher Sandra Bartky is helpful to illustrate this point: 'Any political project which aims to dismantle the machinery that turns a female body into a feminine one may well be apprehended by a woman as something that threatens her best with desexualization, at worst with outright annihilation' (Bartky, 1998: 24). Examining why women migrated, left sex work or refused assistance programmes can only be partly understood by looking at the rational decisions women made. What also needs to be taken into consideration is how these situations related to women's perceptions of 'proper' femininity and sexuality and whether they allowed space for women to take up and juggle at times contradictory positions between being a victim, a sex worker, a mother and a wife.

Conflicting narratives: Force, money, sex and prostitution

The dominant discursive and legal regimes of sex trafficking are organised around the dichotomy 'victim' versus 'whore'. This section examines the discursive positions women took up as a way of countering the 'whore stigma' and of dealing with the 'victims' paradigm. I show that migrant women worked with the victims/whores binary, thereby identifying other women as 'whores' and themselves as not-prostitutes. This recuperation, while it accommodated the normative gender and sexuality roles, also permitted women to negotiate a number of divergent subject positions considered incompatible with the social representation of a victim. In doing so, migrant women exceeded the victim/whore dichotomy and asserted subjectivities that are currently not claimable for undocumented migrant women in third party controlled prostitution.

'Force' versus greed

Having established that such economic factors as the impossibility of making ends meet, the lack of satisfactory employment prospects and the financial needs of families all informed women's migratory projects, in this section I return to the issue of poverty introduced in Chapter 2 and examine what other role, apart from indicating a financial need, poverty plays in women's narratives. Respondents expressed their economic need by framing it in terms of 'being forced' into labour migration abroad. The notion of force is not new to our analysis. In fact, force is one of the key components of the UN definition of trafficking and is seen as a necessary condition for trafficking to take place. However, unlike the way in which the UN Protocol uses the term 'force', women did not use it to suggest that a third party had coerced them into labour migration abroad. Instead, their reference to force indicates an economic pressure or need. It is crucial to pay attention to this divergent use of the term 'force' and not to conflate it with 'force' in the customary understanding of 'trafficking'. This permits us to understand the role that references to 'force' play in the women's narratives.

Through reference to poverty or to 'being forced' by economic need, the respondents distanced themselves from the image of a whore. This mechanism of distancing is evident in women's recurring emphasis on the fact that the money they earned through sex work was not for themselves but rather for their parents or their children. Ester and Kateryna stressed that they were sending money to their respective mothers, Ivana to her husband and Marisa to her daughter. Moreover, the women downplayed the importance of money and called attention to the fact that they were not interested in earning 'big' money. This is how Marisa talked about money:

> For me, money is not important. Today you can have one million and tomorrow you spend it ... it is enough that I have money for my daughter, for paying the rent, for doing shopping, for keeping the child ... I bought an apartment for myself because one never knows what might happen tomorrow. So, if I return to Moldova there is an apartment waiting for me there.

Marisa distanced herself from the financial gain she achieved in sex work by saying that money was of no importance to her and stressed the 'fleeting' quality of it. However, at the same time she stated that she bought a flat for herself and revealed how pleased she was at being able to achieve this. During her first return trip to Moldova, Marisa brought home 5000 USD and proudly displayed to her friends the envelope with 3000 EUR in cash that she received as a Christmas gift from an ex-client of hers (she did not mention that last bit). The money Marisa earned allowed her to improve her family's economic situation and to achieve a certain degree of economic stability for herself, and yet she downplayed this by remarking that she is someone who is satisfied with the minimum amount needed to cover her and her child's needs. In this way, Marisa presented herself as a modest person who had worked in prostitution for the well-being of her daughter.

The demarcation set up between women who do sex work for economic gain and those who are on the street due to economic necessity is taken up in similar terms also by other respondents. Maja, for example, spoke of those women who do sex work as greedy:

> It seems to me that if the girl is young she will have time for everything. One can't buy everything at once. Slowly, slowly, everything comes with time. To have an apartment and a car when one is 20 years old ... I can't imagine that ... I wouldn't do it all at once, fast. Because money doesn't go anywhere, it doesn't run away, so to speak. I would do it slower.

Maja, who expected to work in a cabaret as she had done in Lebanon, but instead ended up in third party controlled street prostitution once she came to Italy, explained that she would not do sex work because she was not interested in earning money the quick way at the age of 20. She also specified that for now the 400 USD, corresponding to the amount she earned in Lebanon in thee months, sufficed for her and her family. Maja perceived women who stayed in sex work as those eager to accumulate money:

> This job ... you can catch a disease, it snows and it rains and you are standing there ... just to earn enough to pay for the hotel or buy something to eat. I don't understand these people. Perhaps, they don't like it but they think, 'Today I don't have any money but tomorrow I can earn some more.' They are dependent on money. It seems to me that they are these sort of people ... they destroy their lives at twenty or twenty five [for money]. Perhaps, there are girls who work for the sake of their children ... I don't know.

Maja asserted that the cost of being on the street is not worth the gain. Women who remained on the street were those who, by being greedy for material goods inappropriate for their age, favoured money over their health and well-being. Being greedy for money, desiring to posses and accumulate consumer goods and prioritising one's own needs over the needs of one's family all function as lines of differentiation between prostitutes and not-prostitutes and position Maja as well as other respondents as part of the latter group.

The mechanism through which women distanced themselves from prostitution is best visible in the case of Ester as her account combines aspects from both examples discussed above. Ester made use of the binary distinction between force and greed in order to distinguish between prostitutes and not-prostitutes and simultaneously identified prostitutes with those women whose main concern is spending their earnings on themselves rather than their families:

> I see the girls that aren't forced to work [on the street] but they do it all the same. Maybe they need to. There are persons who go to clean the toilets: they don't do this thing [prostitution] and it's still a job ... They [the girls on the streets] intend to make money and enjoy it for 2–3 days. When they spent it they go out again. Perhaps, I do not want to judge, they are the ones who get the chance to work on their own, earn some money and leave. They desire to do something good

and they do it in this way, they earn the money ... But, you know, it is easy to go out on the street and stay for an hour instead of working and sweating that money ... If she saw something, she can afford it because tomorrow she is back on the street to earn more.

In the first sentence of the quotation Ester differentiates between those women who are like herself and those who are not 'forced' into sex work. This demarcation is further enforced by Ester's remark that those women who are not 'forced' into sex work but are on the streets nevertheless are driven by the desire to buy consumer goods. They work for a while and then spend the money they earned, then work some more and spend it again. Ester labels this kind of prostitution 'easy' and contrasts it to her own situation. She was 'forced' into street prostitution because her family depends on her financially to pay for her father's medications and hospitalisation. She is hence on the street to do a good deed ('do something good') and this is a 'tough' job. Through this oppositional construction Ester was able to see herself as being different from those women who are after 'easy money', and therefore as a dutiful daughter and a not-prostitute.

While the disavowal of prostitution constitutes the main discursive structure and the meaning of the above quote, the interval (i.e. an opening) present within the quotation suggests that the process of disavowal is not a coherent one but it is riddled with contradictions. This is best visible during the moment of what I call 'suspended judgement'. The sentence, 'There are persons who go to clean the toilets: they don't do this thing [prostitution] and it's still a job' expresses Ester's negative and quite moralistic judgement towards prostitution. Some sentences later, while reflecting on why one would work in prostitution when not forced, Ester points out that those women who do so do it because they are eager for money. However, in between these two affirmations, Ester expresses a doubt: 'Perhaps, I do not want to judge, they are those who got the chance to work on their own, earn some money and leave. They desire to do something good and they do it in this way, they earn the money'. This voicing of a doubt is possible exactly because there is a momentary suspension of moral judgement best captured by 'I do not want to judge'. This doubt opens space for the respondent to reflect on the situation of other women on the street. She shortly considers that those other women might be working independently from a third party, have some kind of project of their own and perhaps 'desire to do something good' too. While one might think that this would lead Ester to think about the similarities between her and other migrant women's situations, this was not the case. As soon as the interval came to an end, the judgement mode took over once again, this time even sharper then at the opening of the paragraph: 'But, you know, it is easy to go out on the street and stay for an hour instead of working and sweating that money.' In this way Ester ruled out the doubt and established herself again as different and therefore not a prostitute.

To interpret women's reference to 'being forced' into prostitution exclusively in terms of brute force fails to take into consideration the function 'force' plays in women's narratives and the formation of women's subjectivities. Contrary to 'whores' who, as Marisa put it, 'are those women who sell themselves for money', respondents framed their working in prostitution as driven by the financial responsibility they had towards their children or parents and not because they were greedy for money or material goods. Women's disavowal of prostitution is hence contingent on their 'being forced' into prostitution. Framing the matter in these terms could be interpreted in terms of women recuperating and strengthening the binary between 'good' women and 'real' prostitutes. However, I think that such a reading would simplify the dynamics at play and miss the point that this differentiation is always already unstable and that it is precisely this instability that enabled women to negotiate the tensions that arose from their attempts to reconcile their own experience of sex work migration and the social and moral values ascribed to prostitution.

I am a moral person, I am a mother and therefore not a prostitute

The tensions that arose from respondents' efforts to negotiate different subject positions become all the more visible when attention is paid to the motif of force in relation to sexuality and, more precisely, sexual pleasure. Women contrasted sexual pleasure in prostitution to that of 'force', by which they meant economic necessity. Ana's narrative offers an example of this when recounting an episode that occurred shortly after she had left third party controlled street prostitution. On that occasion a receptionist at a shelter for undocumented migrants run by a religious organisation threw her out because he suspected she had had sex with one of the male guests. Ana explained the receptionist's decision by saying that he threw her out because he perceived her as a prostitute. She further commented that his impression was wrong because the fact that she had worked on the street had nothing to do with her being a prostitute:

> It doesn't matter that I've worked on the street. I didn't do it because I liked it. I did it because I was forced. ... When one really wants to do this thing, then it is a sin, but when I chose it [thinking] it is enough

that I'm in Italy and once there, I'll then take care of it all by myself ... [then it is different].

As Ana put it, she was 'forced' into prostitution, meaning that she who 'just' wanted to 'get to Italy' had no other option of reaching the desired destination except by agreeing to work in prostitution. In this way, Ana contrasts consenting to prostitution as a means to an end and entering prostitution because one derives erotic pleasure from doing sex work. Other respondents proposed a very similar distinction. When Kateryna spoke of Daniela, with whom she had run away from a third party under whose control they had worked for several months, Kateryna stressed the difference between her own and Daniela's reasons for leaving prostitution. Whereas Kateryna left because she did not like prostitution, Daniela left because she was afraid of not getting paid. Rather interestingly, Kateryna did not mention the conditions in which they both worked. Instead of mentioning the commonalities of their labour conditions or the fact that neither was getting paid, she stressed Daniela's 'liking' and her not 'liking' of prostitution, which in turn allowed Kateryna to distance herself from being a prostitute. Kateryna's framing of why one exits prostitution comes very close to Liudmila's comment that leaving or not leaving prostitution is a matter of individual decision. To paraphrase Liudmila, those women who want to leave the street leave, and those who stay do so because they like money and sex.

By representing themselves as modest and chaste, the women resisted the social representation of the prostitute as a greedy, promiscuous and unworthy woman (Scambler and Scambler, 1997). They searched for ways to counter social stigmatisation. When relating how she felt while working in prostitution, Liudmila voiced this fear of stigmatisation as this: '[When I was on the street] some days I thought that I'll never find a person who will fall in love with me ... that I'll not be able to have a family and children.' In order to counter the fears of stigmatisation women called attention throughout their narratives to their being a mother or a wife. Ivana positioned herself as chaste and a proper wife by stressing how she has always been faithful to her husband and how when younger she never used to have more than one boyfriend at the time. Marisa, on the other hand, emphasised her being a mother and stressed that she was in prostitution because she needed to support her child. Interestingly, Marisa's child never became clearly discernable in her narrative. At times the child was a son, other times a daughter, and from time to time the child was not one but many. The fact that the child was never made 'real' but retained a discursive quality suggests the symbolic authority motherhood yields in countering the stigma of prostitution and in positioning respondents as 'proper' women. Lorraine Nencel's (2000) study of prostitution in Peru remarked that the women she interviewed defined themselves as not-prostitutes because they saw themselves as mothers and hence virtuous. These women identified other prostitutes as 'whores' by stressing their lascivious and promiscuous nature. That sex workers overwhelmingly use the image of a 'good mother' in their accounts of themselves has been also observed by Denise Brennan in her study of independent bar prostitution in the Dominican Republic. In depicting themselves as selfless and caring mothers and in stressing their family obligation and sacrifice, Brennan observed that sex workers contrast mothers and prostitutes and identify with women who are mothers (Brennan, 2004: 147).

Ioanna's case best illustrates how the processes of disavowal and of balancing different subject positions are often contradictory. The respondent, recalling a conversation she had with the adolescent daughter of her Italian boyfriend, recounted how the daughter, who knew that Ioanna has worked on the street, used to ask her questions about 'it' from time to time. Ioanna described her engagement in this conversation like this:

> I told her [about it] in order to make her understand, so that she doesn't think wrong about it. So that she does not think that we came here because we like this. If I would like this, I could also find it at home.

Wanting to make sure that her partner's daughter does not think of her as a 'whore', Ioanna explained that her being in Italy is a result of her desire to migrate rather than a reflection of her desire for sexual pleasure. Reference to sexual pleasure as opposed to 'force' discussed earlier is how Ioanna framed the period she spent in third party controlled prostitution. At the same time, however, she put forward a more complex and unstable account of prostitution:

> I was wearing my skirt down so that my stockings wouldn't show. I kept the stockings always up. I never stood like this [with the mini-skirt up so that one could see the stockings]. During the summer some girls are naked. That's not a way to do things. If she dresses like this, it means this isn't her job. I'm a little bit moralistic person. From time to time, when I go out, I like taking a look at the way

girls are dressed. I feel sorry for them because if they were financially doing well at home they wouldn't be here. If she is half naked
it means there is no work and she has to do like this. Other times
I think that if she dresses like this, she is certainly a whore. At times
I don't know.

This quotation can be divided in two parts. In the first part, ending with
'I'm a little bit moralistic person', Ioanna recalls the period when she
worked in street prostitution, describes two ways of being dressed and
identifies one with the proper way and the other with the improper. The
proper way of dressing (with the skirt not too high up) is opposed to
being 'half' dressed or even naked. The woman who dresses 'improperly'
is described as the one for whom prostitution is not work: 'If she dresses
like this, it means this isn't her job'. At this point, the following question arises: if a woman 'half' dressed standing on the street 'selling sex'
is not doing it in order to earn money, then why is she on the street?
Ioanna offers an answer to this question with 'she is certainly a whore'.
By identifying this woman as a 'whore', Ioanna, whose way of dressing
differed from that of the other woman ('I kept the stockings always up'),
depicted herself as a properly dressed woman and thus not a 'whore'.
Within this discursive framework, dress stands as a visible marker of difference between the 'real' prostitutes and the not-prostitutes.

Yet at the same time, the above quotation shows how difficult it is to
maintain, for someone who has worked in street prostitution, a clear-
cut distinction between prostitutes and non-prostitutes as well as a
coherent identification with the latter category. This transpires not only
from the last sentence of the earlier quotation but also from the sentence about the woman who is 'half' dressed: 'it means there is no work
and she has to do like this'. This phrase explicitly signals Ioanna's doubt
regarding the previously articulated differentiation. The respondent
thus expressed a doubt whether the women she identified as 'whores'
due to their attire may be obliged to wear their clothes in a certain
manner in order to attract sporadic clients. The ambiguity of Ioanna's
positioning in relation to prostitution becomes more evident when she
mentions that from time to time she would do a round to see what
women working on the streets were wearing. After leaving street prostitution, Ioanna was in a habit of returning to the areas she used to work
and approach and talk to women on the streets. She also, to paraphrase
the respondent, gave them advice about how to do sex work. While
doing so, Ioanna never told these women that she herself had worked
in street prostitution. When women asked how come she knew certain

things about sex work, she would reply that she knew it through hearsay. What Ioanna's narrative illustrates rather well is the interplay of the processes of both disavowal and acknowledgement of prostitution. The process of recognition is most noticeable in Ioanna's positioning herself as the one 'in the know' about sex work and therefore as a professional. From this perspective, Ioanna's observation about improper ways of dressing assumes an additional interpretative dimension. Among sex workers, professionalism is conveyed by, among other things, having a regard for one's own appearance and by refusing sexual stimulation and pleasure from clients (McKeganey and Barnard, 1996). In this regard, the remarks Ioanna made about her dress and the distance she took from sexual pleasure can then also be read as claims of professionalism. These considerations on migrant women in third party controlled street prostitution taking up the position of professional sex workers point to the shortfalls both of the dominant rhetoric of eastern European women as naïve 'victims' and of Italian sex workers' dismissing the professionalism of migrant women working in the sex industry (Corso and Landi, 1998: 213–17).

Conclusion

Studies of eastern European women's sex work migration to Canada and Turkey have documented that women did not want to be seen or treated like prostitutes (Gülçur and İlkkaracan, 2002; McDonald et al., 2000). Non-migrant women in street and club prostitution in places as varied as England, Peru and the Dominican Republic rarely claimed the position of a sex worker and were rather determined in refusing such an identification (Brennan, 2004; Nencel, 2000; McKeganey and Barnard, 1996). In this respect, the respondents in my study dealt with the 'whore stigma' similarly to other migrant and non-migrant sex workers in both street and off-street prostitution. Since the discursive structures of prostitution and the legal schemes pertaining to sex trafficking engender and institutionalise the binary distinction between 'whores' and 'victims', women inevitably recuperated and maintained this normative gender binary. Any easy critique of this recuperation needs to take into consideration that for undocumented migrant women being identified as a 'whore' is likely to result in arrest and deportation while being identified as a 'victim' might open an avenue for legalisation of their immigration status and entitlement to rights. Yet women necessarily had to deal with the contradiction produced by claiming subject positions that exceeded or overlapped with the normative binary. This meant that women might identify as victims and simultaneously repudiate the same by putting forward their determination in carrying out their migratory projects or the professional attitude towards sex work.

These kinds of negotiations on the level of identity and the imaginary might be considered symptomatic of 'false consciousness', understood in terms of a disavowal of 'reality'. Such a notion, however, remains largely inadequate in accounting for women's subjectivity, as it relies on problematic approaches to the formation of both social reality and subjectivities. Critiques of classic Marxist notions of ideology have undermined a 'negative' notion of ideology that rests on the assumption of a 'non-distorted' vision of reality. False consciousness works with the assumption, as Stuart Hall puts it, of an 'empiricist relation of the subject to knowledge, namely that the real world indelibly imprints its meanings and interests directly into our consciousness. We have only to look to discover its truths. And if we cannot see them, then it must be because there is a cloud of unknowing that obscures the unilateral truth of the real' (Hall et al., 1996: 52). Instead, poststructuralist accounts of subjectivity have further elaborated on the notion of 'the imaginary', understood following Althusser's classic formulation, in terms of the imaginary relationship of individuals to their real conditions of existence. In other words, the imaginary refers to a set of socially mediated practices that function as the unstable and contingent anchoring points for identifications (Braidotti, 2002).

To view women as victims or sex workers means to position and confine women's lives within the narrow interpretative framework of either oppression or resistance to normative structures and discursive constructions. While this approach is useful to examine and assess the type and degree of agency of migrant women in third party controlled prostitution, it does not offer a more nuanced discussion about how norms and discourses are inhabited, or answer the question as to what makes individuals both identify and resist certain subject positions. In order to explore these processes, there is a need to give space to the tensions and contradictions in these women's lives. Accounting for these contradictions is likely to make our interpretative work more difficult but it will, however, offer an understanding of the constitution of migrant women's subjectivities. Subjectivity emerges through the manoeuvring of contradictory investments and desires in relation to the dominant and prescriptive model of femininity. These imaginary relations, while set up in fantasy, are managed by individuals who are always already culturally and historically located and hence embedded within specific relations of power among which I identified immigration regulations as the key one to consider. Next to emphasising the importance of sexuality and gender in relation to subjectivity, the social positions that women took up and the ways in which they negotiated the tensions such positioning produced, re-arranged or better adjusted the category of femininity, showing that femininity is a set of interactions that women act out in an often contradictory manner across symbolic and social terrains. The challenge women's lives embody then is to rethink how this rearrangement of femininity enables the emergence of new figurations of subjectivity and what space this might be opening for social and political transformations in today's Europe.

5
Conflicts of Mobility: Migration, Labour and European Citizenship

Introduction

In their reflection on the regulation of sex work in today's Europe, Phil Hubbart, Roger Matthews and Jane Scoular (2008) suggest conceptualising sex workers as exemplary figures of new forms of exclusion in Europe. The analysis that the authors undertook of the legislative changes in three different locations, namely the Netherlands, Sweden and England and Wales, prompted them to conclude that despite the different and apparently contrasting laws regulating prostitution in the three countries the outcomes of the law were very similar. Whether the law enforced legalisation of prostitution as in the Netherlands, prohibition as in Sweden or abolition as in the UK, it has invariably repressed first and foremost on-street sex work and displaced it to suburban areas where sex workers are less visible, more isolated and difficult to get to by outreach groups. Consequently, streetwalkers find themselves in situations of greater social isolation and vulnerability to abuse. Geared allegedly towards combating of trafficking, prostitution policies have produced, the authors argue, new and variable geographies of exclusion whereby sex workers end up occupying social spaces which are remote from 'respectable' society and removed from the protection of the law (Hubbard et al., 2008: 149).

The analysis of women's cross-border migration, labour arrangements and subjectivities that I presented in the previous three chapters challenges an exclusion-based model of understanding migration, sex work and citizenship in Europe. In order to convey sex workers' exclusion from the state sanctioned labour markets and the enjoyment of legal protection the state grants to its legal residents and citizens, Hubbard, Matthews and Scoular work in fact with an exclusion-based framework.

The state, the authors suggest, not being able to accommodate sex workers within the boundaries of the social body, displaces them from its polity.[1] In light of my data, it is my claim that an analytic and interpretative model based on exclusion fails to grasp the transformations in governance and political subjectivities taking place nowadays in Europe. This is not to say that whether for reasons of morality or security, EU states do not enforce strict control over migrant sex workers' movement and labour. However, I contend that despite the emphasis it places on social justice and rights of the oppressed groups, the exclusion angle is paradoxically not that different from the viewpoint that sees migrant women in the sex sector as victims devoid of agency. Both perspectives inscribe the mobility enacted by migrant women within a static framework, whether of exclusion or of victims, that divests women's spatial, labour and social mobility of it political significance and that is inadequate if not misleading in conveying the transformations of political, economic and social life in Europe at the present time.

The exclusion-based model works from what we can call 'classical' premises about state borders, division of labour and sovereignty. The 'classical' take on migration conceptualises borders in terms of external edges of the state, labour in terms of gendered division between productive and reproductive work and sovereignty in terms of state sovereignty. Given its reliance on a strict connection between state and its territory, the exclusion viewpoint sanctions a dualistic analytic mode that distinguishes between 'inside' and 'outside', and 'citizens' and 'aliens'. From this standpoint, illegal migrant women working in street prostitution in conditions of confinement imposed by a third party could indeed be taken as paradigmatic figures of exclusion. It is my aim in this chapter to revisit this framework and discuss its limits in light of the data that the foregoing chapters have described. I depart from the interpretative framework based on exclusion in favour of a model of differential inclusion, which brings to the fore the stratification and proliferation of subject positions. My intention is not to compensate the interpretative imbalance in favour of inclusion (although differential) by focusing on the acquisition rather than deprivation of rights. Rather, my aim is to broaden the interpretative scope and political relevance of feminist scholarship by integrating the studies on changes of sovereignty, labour and citizenship as developed in critical political theory into the feminist analysis of migration and sex work in Europe.

In contemporary times, borders, labour and citizenship have all undergone major transformations engendered by migratory movements. By focusing on women's enactment of their spatial, labour and social mobility, I will show that an analytical framework organised from the vantage point of gender and sexuality is best placed to offer a nuanced reading of emerging forms of governing and political subjectivities that do not operate along the inclusion/exclusion or inside/outside model. In the sections that follow, I proceed by discussing the transformation of borders and the delocalisation of control in the EU, and the consequent changes to the EU's political and juridical space. The considerations I develop around the regulation of labour mobility and the heterosexual and patriarchal social arrangements built within immigration regulations bring me to question the adequacy of those viewpoints that see migrant women's labour in the sex sector as an instance of unfree labour or slavery. I further illustrate how the emphasis placed on the notion of victimhood or on poverty, namely on enforced movement and on the economic determinants of migration, conceal the complexities and the conflicts arising from women's enactment of their spatial, labour and social mobility. In the final section and by way of a conclusion, I discuss the urgency of not positing illegality and legality as opposites and of recasting the distinction between 'citizens' and 'aliens' so as to recognise migration as a constituent force in the formation of the European polity (Mezzadra, 2010).

Spatial mobility

Regulation of circulation

The preceding chapters discussed women's cross-border migration and the realisation of their migratory projects. We have seen that before migrating to Italy a number of women had previous experience of cross-border migration to Cyprus, Turkey, Serbia and among other for seasonal agricultural work, petty trade and entertainment and sex sector work. Some had already been to Italy where they worked on three-month contracts in on-street prostitution for a third party. Migration for work in the sex sector that is primarily arranged as a contract with a third party and rarely independent due to the necessity of covering visa and travel costs, organising cross-border travel, making living arrangements and having a person of reference, can be identified as a short-term project that, given the economic, social, and affective investments that characterise it, can hardly be differentiated from other types of women's transnational migration.

Women's migration from 'east' to 'west' Europe for work in the sex industry has emerged next to other forms of work migrations in Europe. The year 1989 and the political changes that followed were decisive for the entry of 'central' and 'eastern' European migrants in large numbers into 'west' Europe's sex industry. In the late 1970s and the early 1980s, Latin American women were the predominant migrant group in the sex industry. Women from Africa arrived throughout the 1980s and in the second half of the 1980s considerable numbers of migrants from Thailand and French Overseas Territories came to work in the sex industry. In 2000 migrant prostitutes are estimated to be 70 per cent of the total sex worker population in 'west' Europe; some 30–40 per cent of these are women from 'east' Europe. Notwithstanding the extent of the phenomenon, the data on 'east' European migration for the sex industry are extremely scarce. For the most part, migrants' presence in the sex industry is subsumed under the framework of 'sex trafficking', which makes systematic research on migration patterns unavailable. From the available data collected by TAMPEP, Transnational AIDS/STD Prevention Among Migrant Prostitutes in Europe Project, we can observe that the existence of already established migrant communities and economic ties between the countries of origin and destination play a role in the composition of migrant sex-work population. In Italy, for example, women originate mostly from Bulgaria, Romania, Moldova and Ukraine, while migrant prostitutes in Greece are mainly from Russia, Ukraine, Albania and Bulgaria. In Spain the majority of sex workers come from Latin America rather than 'east' Europe, but in Portugal large numbers of 'east' European women work in the Algarve, where as part of the informal recruitment schemes, men work in the construction sector and women unofficially in the sex industry. With the process of EU enlargement and changes in visa and immigration requirements, new EU member states became countries of destination for work in the sex industry. Women from the neighbouring countries of Ukraine, Moldova, Russia and Belorussia work in the sex industry in Poland, Hungary, Romania and Bulgaria. Romanian and Bulgarian women also work short term (between one and three months) in Poland and Hungary. A similar pattern is present in relation to the EU countries situated at the eastern border. In the Scandinavian countries, women from the Baltic States and Russia represent the majority of migrant population in the sex sector. In Germany and Austria, most women working in the sex industry come from the 'central' and southern European countries (Brussa, 2002).

   With the exception of citizens of the EU-15 countries who enjoy freedom to take up employment anywhere in the EU, in the EU labour mobility of nationals from new EU member states and of non-EU nationals in particular is highly regulated. As I explained in the Chapter 1, A8 and A2 nationals' access to the EU labour market as a whole is restricted until 2011 and 2013 respectively. Non-EU nationals, except those who are already residing legally in the EU, have no right to free movement and their mobility is subjected to visa requirement and labour quotas. Regulation of circulation in the EU has been achieved via a strengthening of control at the EU's external borders. The intensification of border controls, seen as compensation for the lifting of the internal borders between Schengen states and the formation of an area of free circulation for EU citizens, meant a relocation of control to the EU's external borders and the creation of what has been dubbed 'fortress Europe'. The term indicates the difficulty of accessing EU space whether via official or illegal channels due to the border controls as well as a series of border and visa regulations that the new Member States are required to apply towards the non-member states. These operations shifted the responsibility for border protection and the interception of undocumented migrants from the EU-15 to the new Member States and turned the latter into a kind of 'buffer zone' or into the EU's new migration 'gatekeepers' (Andreas, 2000). What we can observe, therefore, is that the freedom of persons to move between central and eastern Europe and the former Soviet Union gained in the post-1989 period has been changed and re-mapped via the EU enlargement process that has put in place a regime of differential mobility depending on the county's membership status in the EU. Accordingly, areas adjacent to the EU are being organised into spaces that are hierarchically differentiated through a set of devices and measures aimed at governing people's mobility (Rigo, 2007).

New control fronts

As I showed in the previous chapters and as we can see from the above overview of sex related migration patterns, border controls and restrictive visa and immigration regulations, do not prevent people from migrating. Rather, enhanced border controls increase the undocumented modes of travel and raise costs, duration and the likelihood of abuse for migrants. The arrangements women entered in with third parties in order to reach Italy exposed them to the danger of sexual/physical abuse or to detention and deportation by the border police. Having little or no control over the terms of the journey meant that third parties, instead of the women themselves, determined the women's travel routes and the length of travel. Border controls and the introduction of new visa policies in eastern Europe also raised the costs of travel.[2] For example, for women travelling from Moldova or Ukraine without valid travel documents this meant that each border crossing needed to be arranged by an agent/third party and it needed to get paid for. Repayment of travel costs for the previous segment and arranging for the next segment of the journey entailed that at times the woman would get transferred from one agent to another against payment. In other words, each segment of the journey was ascribed a monetary value that the women, having no financial means, were required to pay off though sex work at various locations during the journey. This in turn increased the level of control that third parties exercised over women, both during the journey and upon their arrival at the destination.[3]

While border, visa and immigration regulations did not stop women from leaving their countries of origin and getting to Italy, they did, however, interfere with women's travel. Let me illustrate this through an example, part of which I discussed previously. Kateryna decided to migrate to Italy and used the services of an agency to organise her travel. She left Moldova travelling with a group of ten other women and, having traversed Romania and Hungary by train, was intercepted by the border police while crossing the Austrian border on foot. Identified as a VoT (that is, of coerced migration geared towards labour exploitation), she was 'rescued' and returned home. In reality, this meant that she was first shortly detained at the Austrian border and then moved to another prison in Hungary, and released when she had gathered enough money to self-fund her travel back to Romania (this money was given to her by a migrant from Pakistan who was detained for irregular border crossing). From there, Kateryna eventually returned to Moldova and started searching for a different way to get to Italy, again paying an agency. Some months later, she set off again, this time taking a different route (and again travelling with a group), she crossed Romania, Serbia, Albania and finally reached Italy by boat several months later.

As we can see, the interception at the border, arrest in one location, detention in another prison and then finally release did not prevent Kateryna from getting to Italy. Rather, they made her change direction and prolonged the duration of her journey. Women's cross-border migrations show that border control, denial of entry, detention and deportation do not function exclusively as mechanisms of exclusion as they do not necessarily prevent or stop migratory movements. Rather, they decelerate the speed of migratory flows by momentarily diverting their directionality and regulating the time of migration (Papadopoulos et al., 2008).[4] Time, women's experience of cross-border migration show us, increasingly plays a key role in establishing a flexible regime of differential inclusion that regulates migration and access to EU citizenship. This is best visible in the case of the EU enlargement process and the timing of accession whereby full labour participation of A8 and A2 citizens to take up employment anywhere in the EU has been delayed for a period of between two and seven years after accession (Avery, 2009). I suggest that the category of the VoT mobilises a similar temporality. Constructed as 'white' through their recurring representation as blond- and blue-eyed and through discursive positioning as innocent victims, eastern European women are racially indistinguishable from 'European' women.[5] It is precisely their status as victims that differentiates them from their European counterparts and positions them as being *not yet* 'fully' European. Time therefore operates as a mode of governance organised in historically separate stages where 'not yet' represents the stage of prepolitical and thereby the extent to which subjects have progressed in their movement towards democracy and in their capacity for political participation.[6]

The array of border posts, detours, interruptions and returns that Kateryna and other women experienced along their cross-border journeys signal another crucial point with regard to borders and the regulation of migratory movements. The newly-introduced visa requirement permitting movement between different countries in eastern Europe depending on the degree/stage of their EU membership or lack of it, the multiplication of border controls, and the possibility of getting arrested, detained and deported at different points of the journey, all point to the fact that borders and control have undergone major transformations. The processes of European integration and enlargement have brought about significant changes to the spatiality and the rationale of the border (Balibar, 2009, Walters, 2002). While the early literature on globalisation and borders hypothesised the erosion of borders, recent studies point out the ways in which borders have been diffused, dispersed and networked under conditions of globalisation. Borders are thought of less as being continuous linear structures enclosing a political territory and demarcating a state's external edges, and more as being zones, bands, nodes and filters. Indeed, scholars now talk of a 'virtual border' (Freudenstein, 2001) and 'indeterminate' (Bigo, 2003) and 'technological' zones (Barry, 2006). These changes are referred to in terms of the 'proliferation' of borders and a 'delocalisation of control' in order to indicate that control, once located at the borders, is now exercised by a variety of means and in a variety of locations (Rigo, 2005).

Next to the measures already identified by other scholars, such as readmission agreements, the system of visa regulation, carrier sanctions, detention facilities outside the EU, refugee registration and cooperation with third countries in deportation procedures (Adey, 2009; Franke, 2009), I suggest that the UN Protocol and the anti-trafficking campaigns are all instances of such delocalisation. As far as the UN Protocol is concerned, this is best visible in the third part of the UN Protocol, which under the heading of 'preventive' measures recommends the following measures in order to counter trafficking: control of legitimacy and validity of travel documents, enhancement of border controls and training and intensification of cooperation between law enforcement, immigration officials and other relevant authorities. Anti-trafficking campaigns, on the other hand, primarily developed by the International Organisation for Migration (IOM),[7] intervene in migrants' countries of origin to discourage undocumented migration and, via deployment of victimised and wounded women's bodies and subsequent idealisation of home free of abuse, exploitation and prostitution, suggest that staying at home is the safest option for young women (Andrijasevic, 2007; Nieuwenhuys and Pécoud, 2007; Sharma, 2003).

Issues around irregular migration are not unique to IOM's anti-trafficking campaigns but are instead a central component of a number of IOM's programmes. Among others, IOM gathers information and runs a database on VoTs; assists EU governments in 'repatriation' of undocumented migrants; aids governments in developing measures/schemes to intercept undocumented migration from the non-EU member states into the accession countries, as well as from accession countries into the EU; and provides legal and technical assistance to new and non-EU member states in 'improving' the control of their borders. As for other IOM's work, anti-trafficking campaigns are also developed and funded as cooperation among NGO's in countries of departure and governments of countries of migrants' departure, transit and destination. Anti-trafficking campaigns, part of IOM's overall intervention into regulating undocumented migration, and incorporated into EU's *Common policy fon illegal migration, smuggling and trafficking, external borders and repatriations of illegal migrants*, appear as measures by means of which the regulation of migration is extended beyond the state borders and into new control fronts.

What women's migration alerts us to then is to how the EU attempts to regulate people's circulation as a way of governing spaces no longer enclosed by its external borders and to the importance time plays in the regulation of mobility. Women's cross-border movement and labour migration via non-state sanctioned channels is intervened upon through measures, such as anti-trafficking campaigns, that mobilise a stereotypical gendered representation of 'Other' women as victims and men as criminals, as well as through processes of re-bordering that, as the case of IOM shows best, are less about 'control' and more about 'management' combining heterogeneous domains of personnel, people, data, international cooperation and partnerships (Rumford, 2006). This does not mean overlooking the very real and too often tragic consequences of border policing on migrants' lives but it is to say that however polemically potent the image of 'Fortress Europe' might be, it fails to see that the contemporary ordering of borders transforms borders into zones of innovation in the technologies of government and blurs the distinction between EU's 'inside' and 'outside' (Andrijasevic and Walters, forthcoming; Mezzadra and Neilson, 2008).

Labour mobility

Sex work and the regulation of migrant labour

The rhetoric of 'sex trafficking' as new slavery has emerged in correspondence with a deep reconstitution of economic, cultural and political spheres in the contemporary West, resulting in the transformations of labour relations and labouring subjects, new configurations of sexual life and intimacy and changes in the working of the nation state and its modes of governing. 'Sex trafficking', due to its reliance on a stereotypical gendered imaginary, has been identified as a reactionary discourse that serves to assuage the anxieties about changing national identity and borders that in turn get deflected onto anxieties about morality and sexuality. The latter are a consequence of reconstitution of the family, kinship and intimacy that is nowadays increasingly permeated by the logic of the market and commercially mediated erotic relationships and less premised on permanent intimate and social ties (Bernstein, 2007). 'Sex-trafficking' rhetoric has also been seen as an 'act of statecraft' by means of which, at the time of the consolidation of a comprehensive EU policy framework on immigration and asylum, member states are attempting to gain more control over the scope of EU citizenship and preserve national discretion in matters of immigration and citizenship laws (Berman, 2003).

Similar anxieties, engendered by the reconstitution of labour relations and markets in conjunction with the emergence of new forms of statehood and/or political communities, could be observed during the so-called white slave trade, a phenomenon considered a precedent of today's 'sex trafficking'. Eileen Scully showed that the 'white slave trade' that took place in the second half of the nineteenth century and that entailed the movement of white European and North American women to East Asia and South America for work in the sex sector was triggered by three moments of mobilisation and the migration of large numbers of single males. These were, first, the abolition of slavery, which prompted the recruitment of non-white, indentured labour predominantly from Asia in order to replace the labour of African slaves in the extractive industries such as diamond and gold mining and in large construction projects. Second, the impoverishment of the rural population through colonial economies triggered peasants' migration into the cities, colonial armies or indentured migratory labour in extractive and construction industries. At the same time, the establishment of commerce within colonies resulted in the emergence of wealthy native urban elites in the Western imperial enclaves of Hong Kong, Singapore, Shanghai and New Delhi. And third, the colonial opportunities, new frontiers and colossal construction projects set off the large-scale, long-distance migration of single, wealth-seeking men from Europe and North America to the American West, Australia, South Africa, Hong Kong and federated Malay States (Scully, 2001: 77).

These large-scale male migrations prompted a demand for international sex workers, enlarged regional sex work migration and increased native prostitution. Indentured labourers preferred women of their own race or ethnicity and, due to the existing racial and class/cast hierarchies, white sex workers were 'off limits' for non-Western men. Jo Doezema has therefore argued that the term 'white slave trade' is incorrect since, during its initial phase from 1840 to 1880, women who took part in it were not slaves but rather sex workers from North America and western Europe. These women, due to their race and nationality, enjoyed a privileged social status and had substantial control over their working conditions (Doezema, 2000). This changed during the later phase covering the years between 1880 and 1940 when, following the widening of economic inequalities between core and peripheral regions and the subsequent wage differentials, white women's sex work migration and labour was replaced by low-cost labour performed by native women in more exploitative working arrangements (Scully, 2001).

That the economic, political and sexual spheres are deeply interlinked is perhaps best visible in situations where sex workers are recruited through state-regulated schemes. At the peak time of nation-state building in the colonies, recruitment of prostitutes was crucial for maintaining heterosexual and racial social order, and in disciplining male sexuality and increasing productivity. For example, in the mid-nineteenth century, administrators of one of the British Empire's leading penal settlements on the Andaman Islands in the Bay of Bengal recruited female sex workers with similar racial/ethnic backgrounds to the male prisoners (Hindu,

Sikh and Muslim) and introduced family immigration schemes in order to counter sex between men, encourage heterosexual marriages and maintain a high level of palm oil production (Weston, 2008). Similarly, during the same period, the Indian Government introduced a female quota on ships carrying indentured labourers in the conviction that a greater female presence would stabilise gender relations and increase the economic productivity of indentured male workers (Levine, 2007: 148).

Sexuality and gender are pivotal to the formation and definition of the nation insofar as the reproduction of nationhood and citizenship remain premised on heterosexuality and heteromasculinity (Luibhéid, 2002). Gender and sexuality norms are therefore deeply entrenched within processes of nation state and polity formation and regimes of labour disciplining and regulation. In this respect, immigration policies have been shown to play a key role inasmuch as they impose conditions of marriage and social reproduction based on normative assumptions around the nuclear family, marriage and biological reproduction and in turn establish which subjectivities endanger the nation and which promote citizenship (Manalansan, 2006; Alexander, 1994).[8] The category of the VoT certainly operates along very similar lines, as in order to be granted the resident permit that the Italian state devised specifically for the VoTs, women need to adhere to the programme of social integration/rehabilitation and give up sex work. Yet my data alerts us to another possible reading of the so-called Article 18 for the protection and support of VoTs.

Article 18 is part of the Law 40 of 1990, also known as the Turco-Napoletano Law, which, as a law on immigration, is devised for foreigners and not EU-citizens. While the law applies to the situation of 'trafficking' in all sectors of the economy, it has been specifically developed for migrant women in prostitution and allocated nearly exclusively in cases of exploitation and abuse in the sex sector (Barberi, 2007). Given the fact that prostitution is part of the informal economy and not regulated by the state, I suggest interpreting the provision for the VoTs as a measure through which the Italian state attempts to regulate irregular labour. Let me clarify this. In concurrence with other studies, my data shows that migrant women working in third party controlled prostitution have come to Italy on a three-month contract. Some returned 'home' to return later to Italy again with a new contract and some left third party controlled street prostitution to work independently. My sample is too small to come to any quantitative conclusions, but if we consider that, according to the EUROPAP European network for HIV-STD prevention in prostitution, migrants account for about 90 per cent of prostitutes in

Italy, this gives an idea of the proportions of the turnaround of migrants working in the sex sector.[9] Since prostitution is not considered a legitimate form of labour and migrants working in the sex sector cannot work as self-employed or regularise their status on the basis of sex work contract, they cannot be included in the schemes known as 'sanatoria', by means of which the Italian state periodically regularised large number of irregular migrants working predominantly in the informal sector of its economy. By granting women a residence *and* a work permit in a context where there are no official venues to allocate residency to undocumented migrant women in the sex sector, Article 18 *de facto* regularises, albeit temporarily, a segment of formerly irregular labour.

Precarious labour

The Italian state grants Article 18 residence permits on a six month renewable basis. The permit's aim is to assist 'victims' to exit conditions of coerced prostitution and exploitation. The assumption underlying the permit is that, once 'out' of third party controlled prostitution, migrant women will be able to enjoy freedom of movement or take up a job of their choice devoid of exploitation. Yet, for migrant workers and in particular the undocumented ones, the lines of distinction between free and unfree labour are often hazy. Migrants' labour mobility is, as I have illustrated earlier, restricted and regulated via visa, residency and labour regulations. Moreover, even when they are granted a legal immigration status, that status is not permanent but temporary as the case of the six month renewable permit for VoTs shows well. It can certainly be prolonged for another six months and the advantage of this type of permit, compared to others allocated to migrant workers, is that is not conditional on the work permit, which often binds migrants to a specific employer and/or type of employment.

While these schemes differ from one EU country to another and, for example in Spain, migrant workers on temporary contracts are allowed to take up work only in a specific and highly restricted geographic area, there is a tendency to progress towards a system in which residence permits are contingent on a work permit. This means that breaking the contract with a given employer has direct repercussions on the migrant's residence permit and can lead to migrants becoming illegal if, within six months, as in case of Italy, they do not find a new employer. This shows that the legality of residence and employment do not overlap neatly, and that legality in one category does not necessarily entail legality in the other (Anderson, 2007). Moreover, if a migrant acquires a legal immigration status, this is no guarantee of the permanence of that status as that status needs to be renewed on regular basis. The fact that one can fall 'in' and 'out' of legality goes against states' assumption that illegality is something outside the immigration system and that it can be dealt with through immigration controls and state-regulated labour recruitment schemes.

The temporality of immigration status migrants hold and the limitations they experience due to the restrictions of the work permit with regard to changing the type of employment or employer, result in migrants' temporary employment in both 'formal' and unregulated economic sectors. Women who exited third party controlled street work and stayed in Italy returned to do sex work or, alternatively, found work as domestic workers in private households, cleaners in the public sector, nurses, waitresses, assistant hairdressers and temporary factory workers. Labour mobility of migrant women who left sex work is limited therefore to the low-wage sector and to those jobs to which Liudmila – in the Preface to this book referred to as 'not a real job'. In her research on low-waged labour in the EU and in particular in the domestic sector, Bridget Anderson has found that even those migrant domestic workers who have a legal status or EU citizenship experienced difficulties in moving out of domestic work and finding higher-wage employment. Due to the limitations caused by the gendered and racialised coding of the labour markets, migrant domestic workers in a number of EU countries saw prostitution as the only other work option available to them (Anderson, 2000). Accordingly, the situation of exploitation in third party controlled prostitution cannot be seen as the exact opposite of the legally regulated and protected world of the 'formal' economy. Take, for example, the fact that some factories in northern Italy pay migrants a so-called global salary, namely while paying the contribution to the state as they would for an Italian worker, the wages that employers play to the migrants correspond to those that migrants would earn if working in their countries of origin.[10] Exploitation, and at times deception and coercion, can and do occur within both legally regulated and irregular systems of work and within legal and illegal systems of migration (Rogaly, 2008). This goes to show that migrant women's labour in the sex sector, whether third party controlled or not cannot be seen as the epitome of unfree labour but needs to be examined along with other forms of migrant low-waged labour.

If exploitation, confinement and constraints imposed on migrant labour make a straightforward distinction between free and unfree labour extremely difficult, the task of scholars should be to investigate the conditions and factors that permit third parties and employers to exploit and profit from migrants' labour. Broad characterisation of working relations in the sex sector in terms of debt-bondage or sexual slavery are unhelpful as they tell us little about the political and historic context in which these relations unfold and conceal, as I have shown in Chapter 3, the resources and relationships migrant women develop despite the situation of control and confinement they might be experiencing. In his work on new forms of slavery in the global economy, Kevin Bales identified two forms of slavery that overlap with assumed control modalities of 'sex trafficking', namely contract slavery and debt bondage. Contract slavery, predominant in Southeast Asia, Brazil, some Arab states and parts of South Asia, is a type of slavery in which written contracts are used as a guarantee of employment and through which a person is tricked into slavery where she/he is under threat of violence, has no freedom of movement and is paid nothing. Debt-bondage, common in South Asia, binds a person into slavery through a debt that is not lessened though the slave's labour and that was originally contracted through a loan (Bales, 2000: 463).

Contrary to the importance given to debt in explaining debt-bondage as a key feature of third party controlled prostitution, my analysis has shown that debt did not play a determining role in maintaining the condition of confinement and that women did not give too much weight to the debt. They did not consider themselves to be 'bound' by the debt but instead regarded it as a risk of the trade that concerned third parties alone. As I illustrated in Chapter 3, a possible reason could be found in the fact that women usually did not take loans from third parties. Instead, the latter debited a certain sum to the women in a way that lacked any transparency. As Bales points out, the situation of non-transparency might work in favour of the lender and further trap the debtor, but it might also, I contend, diminish the importance given to debt and its function as a bond that binds the debtor to the lender. Moreover, instead of exercising 'complete control' over women as it is often assumed, labour arrangement between parties and women left space for negotiations and third parties imposed heightened constraints over women's labour for a limited duration rather than binding women by means of debt for an indeterminate period. The identification of third party controlled migrant labour in the sex sector with (sexual) slavery results in the focus being placed exclusively on third parties and in leaving too often out of the view the role residency and employment regulations play in creating the conditions that facilitate control and exploitation of migrant labour. As thereby the state equips third parties and employers with labour control and retention mechanisms, such as in the case of 'global salary' discussed above, that would otherwise not be available to them, subsuming migrant work in the sex sector under the category of slavery sidelines questions of labour rights for migrant workers.

The temporality of immigration statuses experienced by women, as well as the limited availability of jobs which women encountered after they have left sex work and despite having both the resident and work permit, point to the extent to which flexible and precarious labour arrangements are present across both 'informal' and 'formal' sectors of the economy and show that 'informal' and 'formal' labour markets increasingly overlap. Given that legal immigration status is temporary and that in case of its interruption one cannot claim cumulatively months or years of legal residence towards a permanent residency but must start from zero, we can observe the increased difficulty of a 'progressive' legal migratory path that leads to the allocation of permanent residency and eventually of citizenship. The temporality of legal statuses therefore suggests that immigration regulations produce differentiation and stratification of legal statuses and subjectivities rather than straightforward inclusion or exclusion in the labour market. This in turn urges us to consider the increasing breaking apart of the citizen–worker dyad and therefore of the model according to which full-time paid employment constitutes the key prerequisite for citizenship.

Social mobility

Saskia Sassen has identified 'sex trafficking' as a 'counter-geography' of globalisation in that it represents an alternative source of income that relies predominantly on women labour. The centrality of women within these counter-geographies signals a new political-economic reality to which Sassen refers as the 'feminisation of survival' (Sassen, 2000: 505). Investigating ways in which gender matters to capital, examining the reorganisation of the labour markets by paying attention to the incorporation of women's labour and studying the impact of economic restructuring on women's lives are all indispensable in order to understand women's migration in post-1989 Europe, whether for the sex or other sectors of the economy. The implementation of institutional and free-market oriented economic reforms are crucial EU integration criteria and set the schedule for EU candidacy and membership (Iverkovic, 2003).[11] The primacy that the EU gives to its economic agenda in the new member as well as non-EU neighbouring states such as Ukraine and Moldova has been critically addressed for it brought about cuts in welfare and education, and worsened social and economic benefits for women previously in place. The impact these economic changes had on young women's lives and that I discussed in Chapter 2 showed that depending on their age, economic background and existing state of employment all women faced increased economic hardship, lack of employment opportunities and lack of future work prospects. Some could find no employment once they had completed their high school or vocational education and had to earn their living by small-scale buying and selling of goods at local markets. Others, who were studying at the university or already employed could not make ends meet through a part time job as it did not suffice to cover the increase of educational and living costs. This meant that young women's chances of being economically self-sufficient were rather limited and that they experienced difficulty in finding initial employment, improving their economic situation and gaining independence from their families.

While certainly crucial in understanding one factor behind women's migration, a structural and economic outlook on women's migration is however insufficient to comprehend the complexity of subjective motives and desires that inform migratory projects. A feeling of being 'stuck' in life or the desire to find a partner and love are equally important as economic hardship in capturing the reasons why people migrate. Kateryna, for example, dropped out of school first and left for Italy later because of her family's economic hardship and took up work in order to help alleviate her family's economic burden. Yet she also left school because was ashamed by her family's poverty and her father's alcoholism and was angry at her mother's incapacity to leave the circle of domestic violence, find a job and take care of respondent. Her decision was also prompted by being disappointed in herself when she went from being one of the best students in the nation to one of the worst in her class. For Kateryna, migration to Italy was a way out of what she perceived as a series of impossibilities and failures. The other factor not contemplated by a structural approach to migration but gaining importance in migration studies (Mai and King, 2009) and prominent in my data is that of love. The desire to find someone to fall in love with and with whom to establish a relationship was among key factors that influenced several women's decision to move. Some were divorced and with a child and saw few possibilities of finding a partner in their home countries; others were single and had friends who left to work in the sex industry and found a man so they hoped to get equally lucky. The desire to develop new intimate relationships and to move to a place where one can live one's emotional expectations more freely and fully is hence a crucial aspect of women's mobility and of their subjective migratory histories (Alexandrova, 2007; Laliotou, 2007).

That women might not be seen as 'victims' or 'agents' on the basis of whether, *prior* to migrating, they have been 'forced' or 'chosen' to work in the sex sector became visible in the discussion I undertook in Chapter 4 of the contradictory social positions that women took up in the process of negotiating their being migrants as well as sex workers. A subjective level of analysis allows us to see (and grapple with) those tensions and contradictions that indicate that subjects do not occupy one stable and singular position but that they are processually constituted through multiple and often conflicting positionings. Gender difference and sexuality, I have shown, are key in understanding the process of subject formation. This means that subjects do not simply position themselves in opposition to the normative discourses but might at the same time both accommodate and resist, as in the cases of the women interviewed, normative gender roles.

Taking into consideration the efforts, the energy and the expectations that women invested into their migratory projects, it might seem odd that they put much emphasis on being 'victims' both in relation to their Italian boyfriends and the Italian authorities. This accommodation of victimhood, based on the binary opposition between 'whores' and 'proper women' that respondents recuperated and maintained, relieved them of the whore stigma, conferred upon them social acceptance and made it possible to legalise their immigration status avoiding, therefore, the danger of deportation. It moreover permitted women to disavow prostitution and claim socially accepted women's roles such as those of a mother or a wife. And yet, at the same time, women also showed pride in being successful migrants and having achieved some of the goals that drove their projects of migration in the first place such as financially helping out their families, becoming independent from the parents, finding a lover or a partner and improving their prospects more broadly. Additionally, they stressed professionalism and expertise in carrying out sex work and valued positively the effect it had on their sex life and in particular in enabling them to meet their boyfriends' sexual expectations. It is through taking up all of these positions rather than only one that the respondents constituted their sense of self. Far from being de-selved, as radical feminists would have it, sex workers' subjectivities are complex and need to be examined in relation to both discursive regimes and juridical norms that regulate their lives. This entails that migration needs to be examined through subjective experiences of migrants, and that gender difference and sexuality, inherent in all aspects of a migratory project, call attention to the complexities and contradictions of contemporary migrant subjectivity.

Quite paradoxically, then, to get legally identified as a VoT represented for migrant women who left sex work a route to citizenship precisely because it acknowledged them as not-prostitutes. As the status of a 'trafficking victim' needs to get actively claimed and a case made in such a way as to match a specific narrative of violence and abuse, it brings about a conflicting situation produced by the fact that the category of the VoT cannot accommodate women's experiences that exceed the boundaries of the category. This is certainly the case with various types of categorisations, but what interests me here is that the category of the VoT conceals women's claims to citizenship though the logic of rescue and assistance, or what Claudia Aradau has called the 'politics of pity' (Aradau, 2004). Similarly, the references to the enormity of the 'new slave trade' and dire poverty as triggers for migration depoliticise women's desires and demands for mobility by reducing them to a forcefully imposed movement or to a socio-economic logic and consequently reproducing the distinction between masses on the one hand and citizens on the other (Aradau and Huysmans, 2009).

Mobility enacted by migrant women, such as attempting to cross by any means the borders into the EU, escaping conditions of economic and emotional impoverishment in their countries of origin or abandoning confining and exploitative work situations despite states' attempts to limit their movement or control imposed by third parties, is not seen as political; nor are women understood in making a political claim. The notion of the VoT conceals, I suggest, the complexities, contradictions and conflicts that characterise contemporary migrant subjectivity, stratified through regulatory mechanisms and multiple in its social positions, and attempt to manage the multiplicity of movements, belongings and histories that characterise contemporary women's migrations by symbolically reducing them to a single typology of the 'victim'.

To show the tensions and conflicts arising from the containment and regulation of migrants' mobility is not simply a matter of acknowledging migrant women's agency despite the regulatory and normative structures. In light of the trafficking rhetoric and policies that capture women's subjectivities within the image of a victim, affirming women's agency is of pivotal importance if we are to challenge the highly stereotypical representation of migrant women as passive and oppressed 'Others'. Yet the importance of paying attention to the tension and conflicts arising from women's enactment of spatial, labour and social mobility goes beyond identifying migrant women as protagonists of contemporary migration flows or in reading their agency in terms of an opposition to normative institutional structures. It rather goes to show that whether pursued by accommodating or resisting the identification as 'victims', women's demands for social and legal legitimacy expose and defy the existing boundaries of citizenship that fail to recognise migrant women in the sex sector as actors endowed with, and constituted through, the capacity to act. What is at stake then is to conceptualise migration as a constitutive force of European polity and move away from the dialectic of inside/outside that identifies migrants as 'Others' to citizens.

Conclusion

In a recent interview, Marjan Wijers, the former President of the European Commission's Expert Group on Trafficking in Human Beings and one of the founders of the first Dutch-based Organisation against Trafficking in Women (SVT), said that she regrets having pushed the term 'trafficking' onto the political agenda. Having experiences as a feminist activist and a politician that make her one of the most prominent experts in 'trafficking' in women Europe she explained that, with hindsight, she and her colleagues should have abandoned the term 'trafficking' back in the 1980s and gone instead for the term 'forced labour' because 'it is more neutral, it is not morally biased and it looks at exploitation itself rather than the way people arrive to be in an exploitative or abusive situation'. 'Trafficking' in women for the sex industry, she explained further, in practice has been and still is predominantly used by states to legitimise repressive measures against migrants and sex workers rather than to protect them from abuse and secure their rights.[12]

The analysis I have undertaken in this book led me to the same conclusions. Initially conceptualised to make visible the abuses that might occur during the process of migration or as part of labour arrangements, current usages of the term 'trafficking' to indicate situations of slavery, and more specifically sexual slavery in the case of migrant women in the sex sector, are inadequate and might even be counter-productive in terms of addressing the abuses migrants might experience. 'Sex trafficking' and 'sexual slavery' hinder our understanding of the ways in which the interaction of employment and immigration regulations strengthen the hand of third parties and make migrants vulnerable to abuse and labour exploitation. What also remains hidden is the agency migrant women exercise in planning and carrying out their migratory projects as well as the resources and relationships that they engender despite the control third parties imposed on their movement and labour in the sex sector, and the state's immigration policies, which put migrants at risk of detention and deportation. The restrictions that the EU imposes on migrants' movement and the hierarchical organisation of access to its labour market and citizenship, as well as the tension and conflicts that arise from women's acting upon their desire for spatial, labour, affective and social mobility, are all depoliticised though the discourse of 'organised crime' and 'victims'. The highly stereotypical image of the VoT stabilises moreover the anxieties about changing European political structure and labour relations following the crisis of the Fordist mode of production and the integration of the labour markets.

This book however also moves beyond the claim that 'anti-trafficking' measures are deployed to police immigration and penalise sex work. I show that the experiences of migrant women in relation to cross-border travel, labour arrangements in the sex and other sectors, and legal immigration schemes/regulations are indicative of broader transformations of borders, labour and citizenship in Europe. Delocalisation of borders, multiplication of labour and proliferation of citizenship indicate a rupture of the connection between the state and its territory and of the citizen–worker dyad on which are based the logic of inside and outside, the gendered division of labour and the integrative model of citizenship. The transformation in the working of borders has brought changes to the notion of territorial sovereignty, which, understood in classical legal theory as resting on the inseparability between sovereignty and the law, has been ruptured through the process of delocalisation. This has produced a 'discontinuity' in the juridical space and results in what scholars refer to as 'shared sovereignty' (Rigo, 2007) or 'overlapping sovereignty' (Ong, 2006). These indicate that state sovereignty is being transformed through the growing involvement of non-state actors and of public–private contractual networks in the government of migration.

Given the fact that borders and sovereignty do not map neatly onto the territory of the EU, there is a need to question the usefulness of the exclusion/inclusion and outside/inside analytical frameworks. In turn, as in today's Europe illegality and legality are not incompatible but are both in equal measure a structural characteristic of contemporary migratory flows, 'citizens' and 'aliens' are not opposites. 'Irregular' migrants, whom Saskia Sassen called 'unauthorized yet recognized' (Sassen, 2006: 296), are contesting and redefining the borders of citizenship through claims to mobility, residency and employment, which are reshaping the material and symbolic borders of citizenship. An account of the emerging political subjectivities in Europe requires, suggests Engin Isin, that we shift our attention from the question 'Who is the citizen?' to 'What makes the citizen?' (Isin, 2009). This would allow us to see how (irregular) migrants participate in the making of citizenship and how citizenship is contingent and contested. From this perspective, instead of being formalistically defined from 'above', European citizenship is a terrain of struggle constituted through a continuous interaction between subjects' enactment of citizenship and its institutional codification. What we need and what the experience of migrant women urge us to articulate is a 'new vocabulary of citizenship' (Isin, 2009: 368) that, organised from a vantage point that brings together feminist theories of gender and sexuality and critical political theory, is best placed to offer a nuanced reading of emerging migrant subjectivities and of the political transformations these are bringing about. Terms such as 'trafficking', 'sexual slavery' and 'victims of trafficking' cannot be part of that new vocabulary because they are embedded within the discursive logic of victimisation and criminality and in the normalisation of new hierarchies and inequalities in Europe.

Notes

1 Migration and Sex Work in Europe

1. Article 3 of the Protocol defines trafficking as follows: '[T]he recruitment, transportation, transfer, harbouring or receipt of persons, by means of the threat or use of force or other forms of coercion, of abduction, of fraud, of deception, of the abuse of power or of a position of vulnerability or of the giving or receiving of payments or benefits to achieve the consent of a person having control over another person, for the purpose of exploitation. Exploitation shall include, at a minimum, the exploitation of the prostitution of others or other forms of sexual exploitation, forced labour or services, slavery or practices similar to slavery, servitude or the removal of organs.'

2. A second UN Protocol addresses smuggling specifically. The *Protocol against the Smuggling of Migrants by Land, Sea and Air* defines smuggling of migrants in the following terms: '[T]he procurement, in order to obtain, directly or indirectly, a financial or other material benefit, of the illegal entry of a person into a State Party of which the person is not a national or a permanent resident.'

3. A8 stands for the eight countries that joined the EU in 2004. These are Poland, Lithuania, Estonia, Latvia, Slovenia, Slovakia, Hungary and the Czech Republic.

4. This means, for example, that Polish nationals have access to the labour market in the UK but not in Germany.

5. These are Romania and Bulgaria who joined the EU in 2007.

6. Article 2(a): 'a structured group of three or more persons, existing for a period of time and acting in concert with the aim of committing one or more serious crimes or offences … in order to obtain, directly or indirectly, a financial or other material benefit'. Article 3(c) defines 'structured group' as a group in which there is continuity in its membership. A randomly formed group for the commission of the offence is not considered a structured group (Scarpa, 2008).

7. For example, under the guest-worker system, family reunification policies did not allow migrant women, unlike men, to bring into the country of migration their spouses or dependents (Bhabha and Shutter, 1994). Were a white citizen woman to marry a foreign national, she would automatically lose her nationality, as was the case, for example, in the Netherlands until the early 1960s. In cases where the husband was deported, the women and children would also be deported back to the husband's country of citizenship (De Hart, 2007).

8. See http://www.nextgenderation.net/projects/alterglobalisation/esf2006/index.html accessed on 5 July 2010.

9. In order to comprehend better this feminist intervention within the prostitution debate, it important to contextualize it briefly within the genealogy of that debate. As Zatz (1997) points out, the important contribution of abolitionist feminists was to emphasise that prostitution does involve sex and relate it further to the organisation of gender and sexuality (Zatz, 1997). By bringing

to the fore the issue of sex and sexuality, they were responding to Marxist feminists for whom the selling of sexual service is a form of alienation taking place through the exploitative relations of appropriated labour. At the same time they were building on the position of liberal feminism and especially on the relationship between the body, property and labour. A critical reading of the liberal concept of property in the person and prostitution and the way it conceals relations of power and dependence is offered by Brace and O'Connell Davidson (1996: 55–78); and O'Connell Davidson (2002: 84–98). For a critical analysis from a Marxist feminist perspective on the radical feminists' position on prostitution as well as their reading of Marx, see Van der Veen (2000; 2001).

10. The overview of the case can be found at http://eur-lex.europa.eu/ LexUriServ/LexUriServ.do?uri=CELEX:61999J0268:EN:HTML#SM, consulted 23 February 2010.

11. The Directive was adopted on 29 April 2004. European Commission, *(71 Final) Proposal for a Council Directive of the Short-term residence Permit Issues to Victims of Action to facilitate Illegal Migration or Trafficking in Human Beings Who Co-operate with the Competent Authorities*, Brussels: Office for Official Publications of the European Communities, 2002.

12. The English term 'social worker' does not quite convey the meaning of the Italian word 'operatrice'. In the social sphere, 'operatore/operatrice' is usually a flexible and precarious worker who does not have the 'classical' education of a social worker but instead a shorter theoretical education and practical training for a particular type of work. During my undergraduate university years I spent at the University of Trieste (Italy), I trained as an 'operatrice' at the facilities of the ex-psychiatric hospital in Trieste – known for their struggle for the closure of the hospitals, reform of the psychiatric system and affiliation to Franco Basaglia's teachings. The training I received in Trieste opened doors for me in terms of the jobs I was offered, which allowed me to earn enough to cover my living expenses and complete my studies in Modern European Literatures. I worked in a day-care centre for women with psychiatric problems, did home assistance for women with post-partum depression, accompanied young girls to see their parents during prison visits, worked in refugee camps in Croatia during the conflict years and then worked in Bologna's women's shelter on a project aimed at assisting women who have reached Italy though trafficking networks and have worked in street prostitution under the control of third parties.

13. The English translation of the name is The Foundation Against Trafficking in Women. The foundation is based in Utrecht, the Netherlands.

14. The Southern-Eastern route leads across the South East Europe, then Albania and finally across the Apulia coast.

15. The Northern-Eastern route leads across Central Europe, then Slovenia and finally across the Friuli-Venezia Giulia border.

2   The Cross-Border Migration

1. From Bologna's daily newspaper *Il Resto del Carlino*, 18 July 1999.

2. Similarly, the report commissioned by the Home Office in the UK concluded that there is no quantitative evidence available for the UK either for adult or child trafficking (Dowling, Moreton and Wright, 2007).

3. 'Normal' work stands for work other than sex work. All respondents distinguish between prostitution and other forms of work, which they refer to as 'normal' work. I discuss the significance of this differentiation in Chapter 4.
4. This might not be always true. Many people coming from Serbia to the Netherlands in the period immediately following the NATO bombing and sanctions reported that the Austrian Consulate in Belgrade, at that time the only Consulate of a Schengen member state to be present in Belgrade, charged 1500 EUR for a three-month tourist Schengen visa.
5. The respondents report that an agency charges between 360 and 500 USD, depending on the country of departure, for a visa and a bus ticket to Italy. Just for orientation, those respondents who worked as schoolteachers or secretaries in Moldova or Ukraine, earned between 20 and 30 USD per month.
6. However, due to Romania's becoming an EU member state, Romania changed its visa policies and introduced visa requirements for citizens of Moldova.
7. This is not valid for Ivana who was married at the time she reached Italy. However, her account differs greatly from other respondents' accounts since she was trafficked to Italy in the sense intended by the UN trafficking Protocol, namely by use of force and deception, and thus it is impossible to view the departure for Italy as Ivana's migratory project. This, however, does not exclude the fact that the respondent looked at migration with a favourable eye as a way of improving her economic situation and opening up new opportunities.
8. A study of migrant sex workers in the UK comes to similar conclusions in relation to their reasons for migrating. The reasons are interrelated and include, among others: job opportunity; improving one's family living conditions; completion of education; escaping war, homophobia or patriarchy and living more rewarding lifestyles (Mai, 2009b).

3 The Sex Trade

1. The Human Rights Caucus is the umbrella for the following groups: GAATW – Global Alliance Against Trafficking in Women/Thailand; IHRLG – International Human Rights Law Group/USA; STV– the Foundation Against Trafficking in Women/The Netherlands; NSWP – Network of Sex Work Projects/UK and USA; Asian Women Human Rights Council/Philippines and India; La Strada/Czech Republic, Poland and Ukraine; Fundación Esperanza/ Columbia, The Netherlands, Spain; Nab Ying/Germany; Foundation for Women/Thailand and KOK – Network Against Trafficking in Women and Violence in the Migration Process/Germany. (Doezema, 2001).
2. International Human Rights Network gathers, among others: CATW – the Coalition Against Trafficking in Women/USA, Asia Pacific, Africa, Latin America and Australia; MAPP – the Movement for the Abolition of Pornography and Prostitution/France; EWL – the European Women's Lobby; FIDH – the International Federation of Human Rights; Equality Now/USA; the International Abolitionist Federation and Women's Front/Norway; AFEM – the Association des Femmes de l'Europe Meridionale and Article I/France (Raymond, 2002).
3. These positions came close to those of so-called sex radicals, such as Pat Califia, Joan Nestle and Gail Rubin. The ideas put forward by sex workers'

rights advocates and sex radicals were based upon their shared criticisms of sexuality and the self as the unified essence of an individual (van der Veen 2001: 35), dismissal of sexuality as an 'ahistorical natural urge', and emphasis on historical and cultural construction of sexuality (Zatz, 1997: 277–308). Sex radicals associated prostitutes with other oppressed sexual minorities and emphasised the challenge prostitution represents for normative heterosexual sexuality (ibid.). This position has been criticised for the celebratory mode it assumes in relation to the selling of sexual labour as a way of resisting gender inequalities (O'Connell Davidson, 2002), and for glancing over the fact that the vast majority of prostitutes enter sex work in order to earn money and not 'because sex for money turns them on' (Zatz, 1997). Sex workers' rights advocates counter these arguments by claiming that celebratory strategies are crucial in challenging again and again the dominant cultural representation and moral codes surrounding prostitution, and in creating a healing 'counterculture of alternative meaning' (Nagle, 2002: 1177–83). For sex workers' rights advocates this project is intrinsically linked to dislocating social stigma ascribed to prostitution. Stigmatisation limits prostitutes' chances of lessening their dependency upon third parties, improving their working conditions and achieving a greater degree of financial independence.

4. Additionally, the dichotomy 'coerced' versus 'non-coerced' prostitution led to a polarisation in terms of abuses and rights to protection. Those incorporated under 'coerced' prostitution are regarded as victims of human rights abuses and are eligible for state protection schemes. In contrast, those who migrate for sex work fall under the category of 'voluntary' prostitution and in case of exploitative work conditions or human rights abuses are not protected by the UN Trafficking Protocol (Sutdhibhasilp, 2002).

5. The significance ascribed to starting work on the street is most apparent in the narratives of respondents who left – and then later returned – to the sex industry. These respondents gave much more space to a description of street prostitution when narrating their first, rather then second, entrance into sex work. In fact, accounts of re-engagement in prostitution are nearly glossed over and, when they are referred to, it is not to describe the moment of entrance into sex work but to point out violence or some other disturbing episode that occurred while working. The importance respondents – who moved in and out of prostitution – ascribed to the first entry and introduction to street prostitution thus resembles accounts of those respondents whose engagement in prostitution was limited to one sex work 'contract'.

6. Since only two of the respondents stayed the entire length of three months with the same third party (some respondents left street prostitution earlier or were deported by the police; some third parties left or were arrested), and one of them received the sum agreed upon and the other did not, my data does not provide me with sufficient information about the degree to which third parties respected payment agreements. The records collected by an outreach unit active in Bologna on migrant women from fSU and Romania confirm my findings with reference to the length of the contract and specify further that at the end of the three months women could choose whether to collect the ten per cent of their total earnings or stay ten days longer and work for themselves (Calderone et al., 2000).

7. While Ioanna does not specify which movie, the image she entertained is best described in terms of a glamorous prostitute.
8. Phoenix's work distinguishes the individual actions of particular men from the 'practice of poncing' identified as an institutional practice of prostitution.
9. The working rate varies between ten and fifteen clients per working shift, depending on the ability of respondents to negotiate a lower working rate. However, in reality, the working rate was not regulated by the number of clients but by the amount of money one had to earn per shift. Respondents were expected to earn between 600,000 lit (approximately 300 EUR) and 700,000 lit (approximately 350 EUR) per shift, with a fee for car service amounting to 50,000 lit (approximately 25 EUR). The respondents could thus lower their working rate in the case where the clients paid them more than the standard fee.
10. She was not accused of having had sex with someone in particular, but 'just' of having had sex and was expelled from the institution. The accusations were made by an employee who saw a condom cover in Ana's garbage can. Even though she explained that, having had nothing else, she used the condom to tie up her hair together in a knot, she was expelled on the basis of being immoral. This example points to the persistent stigmatisation of women who engage in sex work.
11. On the basis of data gathered it is impossible to establish if there is a correspondence between travel, accommodation and visa costs on the one hand, and the total amount of the debt on the other. The respondents were usually informed that they have been 'bought' for a sum varying between 1000 and 2500 EUR but they were not informed about the exact breakdown of expenses. It is certain that travel, accommodation and visa costs made up a part of the debt, but it is unclear what other fees/interests might be added on top of it.
12. The third party settled a 70%–30% deal with Larisa: 70% for the third party and 30% for Larisa. However, since Larisa made little money during that month (i.e. 2000 EUR in one month) the deal was revised in order for Larisa to be able to cover food and accommodation expenses.
13. While this might appear a high quota, a research on independent street work in a working class neighbourhood of Lima found that that sex workers 'had' approximately 15 clients per (day) shift (Nencel, 2000). The same research has shown that the number of clients per shift was proportional to class relations: in a 'higher' class setting, sex workers charged more and thus earned more, even though they 'had' fewer clients per shift.
14. 'Cento' was the price of the sexual service in a room and 'cinquanta' in the car. The prices are in Italian liras and correspond approximately to 50 and 25 EUR respectively.
15. Paradoxically, the respondent said that the clients appeared to be much more scared of catching flu and they would not 'go with her' if was coughing. The fact that some clients purchase unprotected sexual services is explained by O'Connell Davidson as the 'eroticization of risk': 'For such men it is clearly not enough to play the internal game of risk with fantasized dangers. To experience excitement and a subsequent sense of triumph and mastery, these men need to pit themselves against real world dangers, against people and events that are truly outside their control' (1998: 155). O'Connell Davidson

demonstrates that different clients derive different degrees of excitement from this kind of risk. She points out that her interpretation particularly concerns Western men who are regularly exposed to public health campaigns about the importance of safe sex and the danger of AIDS and STDs.

16. The fact that the respondent was isolated and feared further violence allowed the pimp to extract an extremely high amount of labour and profit. Initially, the respondent was instructed to sell sex to 14 clients per night. Later, she was pushed to raise the number to 20. After she succeeded in selling sex to 20 clients, the pimp requested that she prostitute for a minimum 20 clients per night.

17. The interesting aspect of this quote lay in the way in which the respondent objectifies the client: the narrative is framed in a way to depict him as old and asexual, and to suggest that it is Kateryna who was doing him a favour (and not vice versa). Yet the plot is a quite different one: she needed money in order to leave prostitution that night, he suggested going to a hotel room, he volunteered the amount of money, gave her extra money, took the respondent and a peer worker to the train station and bought them tickets to Turin. The implications of objectifications of clients and its meaning in relation to women's subjectivity will be discussed in Chapter 4.

18. My data point to the fact that clients were familiar with the mainstream representation of migrant women in prostitution in terms of helpless victims. In fact, during the fieldwork I learned of clients who 'helped' respondents exactly because they identified them with portraits of young, fragile and helpless women dominant in the mass media discourse in Italy.

4   Multiple Scripts

1. Women countered the objectification by belittling the clients, especially when it came to their appearance (Nencel, 2000). Another means of doing this was to distance themselves emotionally from the clients or even objectify and depersonalise them by focusing on the money (McKeganey and Barnard, 1996).

2. The term 'disappear' is commonly used in counter-trafficking campaign in order to indicate all those women who went abroad and of whom any track has been lost. These campaigns imply or at times state explicitly that these disappearances are caused by the traffickers who kidnap or even murder migrant women. I am not questioning that these brutal and criminal acts happen and that the perpetrators should be severely punished in the court of law, but I am suggesting thinking though the fact that stigma and social judgements on prostitution play a part in rupturing migrant women's relationships to their home communities and that 'disappearing', as the respondent suggests, might at the time be a way of coping with societal exclusion caused by disclosure of woman's work in prostitution.

3. While in the past immigration officials have raised doubts with regard to the misuse of the Article 18 residency permit, namely that women might take advantage of it and apply for the permit in great numbers, this speculation has been refuted by the data showing a highly contained number of applications

for Article 18 permit. For example, in 2006, 1234 women applied and 927 of those obtained the residence permit (Barbieri, 2007; Pearson, 2002).

5 Conflicts of Mobility

1. The authors make use of the work of the Italian philosopher Giorgio Agamben to describe the situation of sex workers in Europe in terms of 'exceptionality' and 'abandonment', both terms used by Agamben in his discussion of refugees and camps. Exceptionality or, more precisely, the 'state of exception' is a Schmittian notion reformulated by Agamben in order to signify a decision, enforced by the sovereign, to place (or 'abandon', in Agamben's terms) certain subjects outside the boundaries of the polis and hence beyond the protection or recourse to the law (Agamben, 1998). The camp stands as for a material spatial manifestation of the abstract juridical dimension that is the state of exception in which, through the suspension of the normal rule of law, the category of citizen is no longer operative and in which the individual is divested of all rights and placed in the state of 'bare life'. Agamben takes the figure of the refugee as paradigmatic of the condition in which the rights of an individual are derogated and in which she/he is made vulnerable to acts of extreme violence and ill-treatment with impunity. The Agambenian framework has been most influential in the scholarly discussion on detention camps for irregular migrants. Scholars have investigated detention camps and the practices enacted within these as manifestations of nation states' sovereign power to suspend the normal rule of law through the state of exception, which immobilises the 'outside' within its borders and abandons those detained in a juridical void (Diken and Bagge Laustsen, 2006; Papastergiadis, 2006; Perera, 2002).
2. Similarly, Rhacel Salazar Parreñas shows that the fee that agencies charged for assisting migrants with undocumented migration from the Philippines into Italy doubled to 8000 USD in the 1990s when Italy joined Schengen and strengthened controls at its external borders (Parrenas, 2001).
3. Scholars approaching 'trafficking' from the perspective of organised crime suggest that, quite paradoxically, increased control over migrants' mobility is likely not to curb transnational crime but rather to heighten the involvement in such organised crime due to the increased profit from 'trafficking' activities (Koslowski, 2001).
4. The notion of time and duration with regard to migration is developed by Dimitris Papadopoulos, Niamh Stephenson and Vassilis Tsianos in their analysis of the working of detention camps in the Aegean zone (2008). Using Paul Virilio's work to re-think the camps from below rather than positing them as a paradigmatic incarceration locale, the authors suggest re-thinking the camps in terms of the 'speed boxes' that regulate the time of migration by decelerating the speed of migratory flows. Within this dynamic framework, detention camps acquire a temporary nature and are conceptualised as provisional stations along multiple migratory routes: migrants are detained, released and they move on.
5. This is best visible in anti-trafficking campaigns. For an overview of anti-trafficking campaigns in eastern Europe and for a detailed discussion on

representational strategies, see my earlier work titled 'Beautiful Dead Bodies' (Andrijasevic, 2007).

6. The notion of time is of extreme relevance for constitution of the political. An important contribution for rethinking the stagiest/historicist distinction between the premodern, namely prepolitical, and the modern has been developed from a postcolonial perspective by subaltern studies that have examined the role of 'not yet' in the government of the colonies and in measuring the achievement of political modernity (Chakrabarty, 2000).

7. The IOM was founded in 1951, the same year as the United Nations High Commissioner for Refugees (UNHCR). Initially called Provisional Intergovermental Committee for the Movement of Migrants from Europe, it was the product of a Belgian and US initiative (Bojcun, 2005). The European Union's Perspectives on the Ukrainian-Russian Border, Eurozine. However, unlike UNHCR, IOM was based on economic rather than humanitarian principles. It has grown quite significantly in recent years and now boasts a total of 127 member states, and a programme budget for 2008 that exceeds 1 billion USD. This sum funds nearly 7000 staff serving in more than 450 field offices in more than 100 countries. It now operates in four main areas of what it calls 'migration management': migration and development, facilitating migration (IOM, 2009).

8. An example can be found in the late 1800s, when the so-called Page Law, which in the first instance targeted Asian women migrating for sex work, restricted Chinese women entering the US as it effectively conflated Chinese women's migration with enslaved prostitution (Luibneid, 2002).

9. Estimates available at http://www.europap.net. 10 March 2010.

10. This information was communicated via email by Paola Rudan to Kanak Attak mailing list on 5 August 2003.

11. One major consequence was the relocation of parts of the production process from western Europe to central and eastern Europe, southern Europe and Turkey enabled through so-called outward processing trade arrangements made between the EU and the 'third countries'. The joining of the EU by the new members in 2004 and the adoption of the EU's external trade agreements, lead to an increased cross-border outsourcing and subcontracting (Smith et al., 2009). Among non-EU member states, the EU liberalised in particular its economic and trading relationship with Ukraine as part of EU's European Neighbourhood Policy (ENP). Women's labour, especially in reproductive or low-paid industrial sector in national economies, is pivotal for the economic restructuring. This is best visible with respect to liberalisation of trade, relocation of production and the subsequent creation of export processing zones (EPZs). In EPZs, boasting special incentives for foreign investors, imported materials undergo a certain degree of processing and are then (re-) exported again. Transnational corporations are able to maintain low wages for male workers in EPZs by relying on largely unmonetised women's reproductive labour and subsistence farming. EPZs are also one of the major sources of formal sector employment for women (ILO, 2002). Manufacturing production, textile and electronic industries in free trade zones rely predominantly on women's labour. By employing (young) low-paid workers and prohibiting unionising, firms secure competitive prices on re-imported goods for the core market in the EU.

12. Interview was conducted by P. G. Macioti as part of the Enacting European Citizenship research project (ENACT), run by the Open University. The project aimed at developing a new take on citizenship in Europe. The project examined in particular sex workers' mobilisation in Europe and its relationship to European citizenship (Andrijasevic et al., 2010).

References

Adam, B. (2002) 'The Gendered Time Politics of Globalization: Of Shadowlands and Elusive Justice'. *Feminist Review*, 70, 3–29.

Adey, P. (2009) 'Facing Airport Security: Affect, Biopolitics, and the Preemptive Securitisation of the Mobile Body. *Environment and Planning D: Society and Space*, 27, 272–96.

Agamben, G. (1998) *Homo Sacer: Sovereign Power and Bare Life*, Stanford CA, Stanford University Press.

Alexander, J. M. (1994) 'Not Just (Any) Body can be a Citizen: The Politics of Law, Sexuality and Postcoloniality in Trinidad and Tobago and the Bahamas'. *Feminist Review*, 48, 5–23.

Alexandrova, N. (2007) 'The Topos of Love in Life-Stories of Migrant Women', in L. Passerini, D. Lyon, E. Capussotti and I. Laliotou (Eds) *Women Migrants from East to West: Gender, Mobility, and Belonging in Contemporary Europe*. New York, Oxford; Berghahn.

Anderson, B. (2000) *Doing the Dirty Work?: The Global Politics of Domestic Labour*, London, Zed Books.

Anderson, B. (2007) 'Battles in Time: The Relation between Global and Labour Mobilities. *COMPAS working papers; No. 55*. Oxford, Centre on Migration Policy and Society.

Anderson, B. and O'Connell Davidson, J. (2003) *Is Trafficking in Human Beings Demand Driven? A Multi-Country Pilot Study*, Geneva, International Organization for Migration.

Anderson, B. and Ruhs, M. (2008) *A Need for Migrant Labour? A Micro-level Determinants of Staff Shortages and Implications for a Skills Based Immigration Policy*. London, Migration Advisory Committee (MAC).

Andreas, P. (2000) 'Introduction: The Wall after the Wall', in P. Andreas and T. Snyder (Eds) *The Wall Around the West: State Borders and Immigration Controls in North America and Europe*. New York, Rowman & Littlefield.

Andrijasevic, R. (2007) 'Beautiful Dead Bodies: Gender, Migration and Representation in Anti-Trafficking Campaigns'. *Feminist Review*, 24–44.

Andrijasevic, R. (2009) 'Sex on the Move: Gender, Subjectivity and Differential Inclusion'. *Subjectivity*, 29, 389–406.

Andrijasevic, R., Aradau, C., Huysmans, J and Squires, V. (2011) Unexpected Citizens: Sex Work, Mobility, Europe. *Environment and Planning D: Society and Space*.

Andrijasevic, R. and Walters, W. (forthcoming) 'The International Government of Borders'. *Environment and Planning D: Society and Space*.

Anthias, F. and Lazaridis, G. (Eds) (2000) *Gender and Migration in Southern Europe: Women on the Move*, Oxford, Berg.

Aoyama, K. (2009) *Thai Migrant Sexworkers: From Modernisation to Globalisation*, Basingstoke, Palgrave Macmillan.

Apap, J. (2001) 'Reshaping Europe's Borders: Challenges for EU Internal and External Policy', in Apap, J. (Ed.) *Report & Policy Recommendations from the*

Conference on New European Borders and Security Cooperation. Brussels, Centre for European Policy Studies.

Aradau, C. (2004) 'The Perverse Politics of Four-Letter Words: Risk and Pity in the Securitisation of Human Trafficking'. *Millennium: Journal of International Studies*, 33, 251–77.

Aradau, C. (2008) Rethinking Trafficking in Women. Politics Out of Security, London, Macmillan Palgrave.

Aradau, C. and Huysmans, J. (2009) 'Mobilising (Global) Democracy: A Political Reading of Mobility between Universal Rights and the Mob'. *Millennium – Journal of International Studies*, 37, 583–604.

Aronowitz, A. A. (2009) *Human Trafficking, Human Misery. The Global Trade in Human Beings*, Westport and London, Praeger.

Augustin, L. (2007) *Sex at the Margins*, London, Zed Books.

Avery, G. (2009) 'Uses of Time in the EU's Enlargement Process'. *Journal of European Public Policy*, 16, 256–69.

Bales, K. (2000) 'Expendable People: Slavery in the Age of Globalization'. *Journal of International Affairs*, 53, 461–84.

Balibar, É. (2009) 'Europe as Borderland'. *Environment and Planning D: Society and Space*, 27, 190–215.

Barberi, A. (2007) 'Dati e riflessioni sui progetti di protezione sociale ex art. 18 dal 2000 al 2006. Segreteria tecnica per l'attuazione dell'art. 18 T. U. sull'immigrazione'. Marzo 2007.

Barry, A. (2006) 'Technological Zones'. *European Journal of Social Theory*, 9, 239–53.

Barry, K. (1995) *The Prostitution of Sexuality*, New York, London; New York University Press.

Becker-Schmidt, R. (2002) 'Introduction', in Becker-Schmidt, R. (Eds) *Gender and Work in Transition: Globalization in Western, Middle and eastern Europe*, Opladen, leske+budrich.

Berman, J. (2003) '(Un)Popular Strangers and Crisis (Un)Bounded: Discourses of Sex-Trafficking, the European Political Community and the Panicked State of the Modern State'. *European Journal of International Relations*, 9, 37–86.

Bernstein, E. (2007) *Temporarily Yours: Intimacy, Authenticity, and the Commerce of Sex*, Chicago, London; University of Chicago Press.

Bhabha, J. and Shutter, S. (Eds) (1994) *Worlds Apart: Women under Immigration, Nationality, and Refugee Law*, Stoke on Trent, Trentham Books.

Bigo, D. (2003) 'Criminalization of "Migrants": The Side Effect of the Will to Control the Frontiers and the Sovereign Illusion'. *Irregular Migration and Human Rights Conference*. Centre for European Law and Integration, University of Leicester.

Bojcun, M. (2005) 'The European Union's Perspectives on the Ukrainian-Russian Border'. Eurozine.

Bosniak, L. (2007) 'Citizenship, Noncitizenship and the Status of Foreign Domestic', in S. K. V. Walsum and T. Spijkerboer (Eds) *Women and Immigration Law*, Abingdon, Routledge-Cavendish.

Brace, L. and O'Connell Davidson, J. (1996) 'Desperate Debtors and Counterfeit Love: Hobbesian World of Sex Tourists'. *Contemporary Politics*, 2, 55–78.

Braidotti, R. (2002) *Metamorphoses: Towards a Materialist Theory of Becoming*, Cambridge, Published by Polity Press in association with Blackwell Publishers.

Brennan, D. (2004) *What's Love Got To Do with It? Transnational Desires and Sex Tourism in the Dominican Republic*, Durham and London, Duke University Press.

Bruinsma, G. and Meershoek, G. (1999) 'Organized Crime and Trafficking in Women from eastern Europe in the Netherlands', in P. Williams (Ed.) *Illegal Immigration and Commercial Sex: The New Slave Trade*, London and Portland, Frank Cass.

Brunovskis, A. and Surtees, R. (2007) *Leaving the Past Behind? When Victims of Trafficking Decline Assistance*, Oslo, Fafo.

Brussa, L. (2002) TAMPEP 5 Final Report, Amsterdam, TAMPEP.

Calderone, B., Farini, D. and Marcasciano, P. (2000) *Tra la via Emilia e ... l'est. L'esperienza del Moonlight Project a Bologna*, Bologna, Comune di Bologna. Settore Socio Sanitario e Bologna sicura.

Caldwell, G., Galster, S., Kanics, J. and Steinzor, N. (1999) 'Capitalizing on Global Economies: The Role of Russian Mafia in Trafficking in Women for Forced Prostitution', in P. Williams (Ed.) *Illegal Immigration and Commercial Sex: The New Slave Trade*, London and Portland, Frank Cass.

Carchedi, F. (2003) 'Le modalità di sfruttamento coatto e la prostituzione mascherata', in F. Carchedi, G. Mottura and E. Pugliese (Eds) *Il lavoro servile e le nuove schiavitù*, Milano, FrancoAngeli.

Caritas/Migrantes (2005) *Immigrazione: Dossier Statistico 2005*, Rome, Edizioni IDOS.

Chakrabarty, D. (2000) *Provincialising Europe. Postcolonial Thought and Historical Difference*, Princeton, Oxford; Princeton University Press.

Corso, C. and Landi, S. (1998) *Quanto vuoi? Clienti e prostitute si raccontano*, Firenze, Giunti.

Corso, C. and Trifiro', A. (2003) *... e siamo partite! Migrazione, tratta e prostituzione straniera in Italia*, Firenze, Giunti.

Crowhurst, I. (2007) 'Socio-Political and Legal Representations of Migrant Women Sex Labourers in Italy. Between Discourse and Praxis', in S. K. V. Walsum and T. Spijkerboer (Eds) *Women and Immigration Law: New Variations on Classical Feminist Themes*, Abingdon, Routledge-Cavendish.

De Genova, N. (2002) 'Migrant "Illegality" and Deportability in Everyday Life'. *Annual Review of Anthropology*, 31, 419–47.

De Hart, B. (2007) 'The Right to Domicile of Women with Migrant Partner in European Immigration Law', in S. K. V. Walsum and T. Spijkerboer (Eds) *Women and Immigration Law: New Variations on Classical Feminist Themes*, Abingdon, Routledge-Cavendish.

Delacoste, F. and Alexander, P. (1988) *Sex Work: Writings by Women in the Sex Industry*, London, Virago Press.

Della Giusta, M., Di Tommaso, M. L. and Strøm, S. (2008) *Sex Markets: A Denied Industry*, London, Routledge.

Diken, B. and Bagge Laustsen, C. (2006) 'The Camp'. *Geografiska Annaler: Series B, Human Geography*, 88, 443–52.

Doezema, J. (1998) 'Forced to Choose. Beyond the Voluntary v. Forced Prostitution Dichotomy', in K. Kempadoo and J. Doezema (Eds) *Global Sex Workers. Rights. Resistance, and Redefinition*, New York and London, Routledge.

Doezema, J. (1999) 'Who Gets to Choose? Coercion, Consent and the UN Trafficking Protocol'. http://www.walnet.org/csis/papers/doezema-choose.html.

Doezema, J. (2000) 'Loose Women or Lost Women. The Re-Emergence of the Myth of "White Slavery" in Contemporary Discourses of "Trafficking in Women". *Gender Issues*, 18, 23–50.

Doezema, J. (2001) 'Ouch! Western Feminists' "Wounded Attachments" to the "Third World Prostitute"'. *Feminist Review*, 67, 16–38.

Dowling, S., Moreton, K. and Wright, L. (2007) *Trafficking for the Purposes of Labour Exploitation: A Literature Review*, London, Home Office.

Ebbe, N. I. O. (2008) 'The Nature and Scope of Trafficking in Women and Children', in N. I. O. Ebbe and K. D. Das (Eds) *Global Trafficking in Women and Children*, London and New York CRC Press, Taylor and Francis Group.

Finckenauer, J. and Schrock, J. (2003) 'Human Trafficking: A Growing Criminal Market in the US', in T. A. Troubnikoff (Ed.) *Trafficking in Women and Children: Current Issues and Developments*, New York, Nova Science Publishers.

Franke, M. F. N. (2009) 'Refugee Registration as Foreclosure of the Freedom to Move: The Virtualisation of Refugees' Rights with Maps of International Protection'. *Environment and Planning D: Society and Space*, 27, 175–380.

Freudenstein, R. (2001) 'Río Odra, Río Buh: Poland, Germany, and the Borders of Twenty-First-Century', in P. Andreas and T. Snyder (Eds) *The Wall Around the West: State Borders and Immigration Controls in North America and Europe*, New York, Rowman & Littlefield.

Gallagher, A. (2001) 'Human Rights and the New UN Protocols on Trafficking and Smuggling: A Preliminary Analysis'. *Human Rights Quarterly*, 23, 975–1004.

GAO (2006) *Human Trafficking: Better Data, Strategy and Reporting Needed to Enhance US Anti-Trafficking Efforts Abroad*, Washington DC, United States Government Accountability Office.

Gülçür, L. and İlkkaracan, P. (2002) 'The "Natasha Experience": Migrant Sex Workers from Former Soviet Union and eastern Europe in Turkey'. *Women's Studies International Forum*, 25, 411–21.

Hall, S., Morley, D. and Chen, K.-H. (1996) *Stuart Hall: Critical Dialogues in Cultural Studies*, London, Routledge.

Harding, S. (1991) *Whose Science? Whose Knowledge? Thinking from Women's Lives*, Milton Keynes, Open University Press.

Hondagneu-Sotelo, P. (2001) *Domestica: Immigrant Workers Cleaning and Caring in the Shadown of Affluence*, Berkeley, University of California Press.

Hubbard, P., Matthews, R. and Scoular, J. (2008) 'Regulating Sex Work in the EU: Prostitute Women and the New Spaces of Exclusion', *Gender, Place, and Culture*, 15, 137–52.

IHF (2000) *Women 2000: An Investigation into the Status of Women's Rights in Central-eastern Europe and the Newly Independent States*, Vienna, International Helsinki Federation for Human Rights.

ILO (2002) *Employment and Social Policy in Respect of Export Processing Zones (EPZs)*, Geneva, International Labour Office.

IOM (2009) *The International Organization for Migration in Brief*, December 2009.

Isin, E. (2009) 'Citizenship in Flux: The Figure of the Activist Citizen'. *Subjectivity*, 29, 367–88.

Iverkovic, I. (2003) 'Fragmentation and Globalization: Yugoslav Successor States and European Integration Process'. BASEES Annual Conference. Hatfield College, University of Durham.

Jeffreys, S. (1997) *The Idea of Prostitution*, North Melbourne, Vic., Spinifex.

Kapur, R. (2004) *Erotic Justice: Law and the New Politics of Postcolonialism*, London, GlassHouse, 2005.

Kapur, R. (2005) 'Travel Plans: Border Crossings and the Rights of Transnational Migrants'. *Harvard Human Rights Journal*, 18, 108–38.

Kapur, R. (2008) 'Migrant Women and the Legal Politics of Anti-Trafficking Interventions', in S. Cameron and E. Newman (Eds) *Trafficking in Human$. Social, Cultural and Political Dimensions*, Tokyo, United Nations University Press.

Kligman, G. and Limoncelli, S. (2005) Trafficking in Women after Socialism: To, Through, and From Eastern Europe. *Social Politics*, 12, 118–140.

Kofman, E., Phizacklea, A., Raghuram, P. and Sales, R. (2000) *Gender and International Migration in Europe: Employment, Welfare, and Politics*, London, Routledge.

Koncz, K. (2002) 'The Gender-Specific Division of Labour in Hungary Since the Regime Change', in R. Backer-Schmidt (Ed.) *Gender and Work in Transition: Globalization in Western, Middle and eastern Europe*, Opladen, leske+budrich.

Koslowski, R. (2001) 'Economic Globalization, Human Smuggling, and Global Governance', in D. Kyle and R. Koslowski (Eds) *Global Human Smuggling. Comparative Perspectives*, Baltimore and London, The John Hopkins University Press.

Kyle, D. and Koslowski, R. (Eds) (2001) *Global Human Smuggling: Comparative Perspectives*, Baltimore and London, The John Hopkins University Press.

Laliotou, I. (2007) '"I Want to See the World": Mobility and Subjectivity in the European Context', in L. Passerini, D. Lyon, E. Capussotti and I. Laliotou (Eds) *Women Migrants from East to West: Gender, Mobility and Belonging in Contemporary Europe*,New York, Oxford; Berghahn.

Lazaridis, G. (2001) 'Trafficking and Prostitution: The Growing Exploitation of Migrant Women in Greece'. *The European Journal of Women's Studies*, 8, 67–102.

Leidholdt, D. (1999) Position Paper for the Coalition Against Trafficking in Women. Special Seminar of Trafficking, Prostitution and the Global Sex Industry, United Nation's Working Group on Contemporary Form of Slavery. Geneva Coalition Against Trafficking in Women, International Movement Against Discrimination and Racism, International Human Rights Law Group and Anti-Slavery.

Leman, J. and Janssens, S. (2008) 'The Albanian and Post-Soviet Business of Trafficking Women for Prostitution: Structural Developments and Financial Modus Operandi'. *European Journal of Criminology*, 5, 433–51.

Levine, P. (2007) *The British Empire: Sunrise to Sunset*, Harlow, Longman.

Lister, R. (2004) 'Citizenship and Gender', in K. Nash and A. Scott (Eds) *Blackwell Companion to Political Sociology*, Oxford Blackwell.

Luibhéid, E. (2002) *Entry Denied: Controlling Sexuality at the Border*, Minneapolis, University of Minnesota Press.

Mahmood, S. (2005) *Politics of Piety: The Islamic Revival and the Feminist Subject*, Princeton, Oxford; Princeton University Press.

Mai, N. (2009a) 'Between Minor and Errant Mobility: The Relation between the Psychological Dynamics and the Migration Patterns of Young Men Selling Sex in the EU'. *Mobilities*, 4, 349–66.

Mai, N. (2009b) *Migrant Workers in the UK Sex Industry: Final Policy-Relevant Report*. London, London Metropolitan University.

Mai, N. and King, R. (2009) 'Introduction: Love, Sexuality and Migration. Mapping the Issue(s)'. *Mobilities*, 4, 293–307.

Maluccelli, L. (2001) 'Tra schiavitù e servitù: biografie femminili in cerca di autonomia', in G. Candia and F. Carchedi (Eds) *Da vittime a cittadine. Percorsi di uscita dalla prostituzione e buone pratiche di inserimento sociale e lavorativo*, Roma, Ediesse.

Manalansan, M. F. (2006) 'Queer Intersections: Sexuality and Gender in Migration Studies'. *International Migration Review*, 40, 224–49.

Marazzi, C. (2007) 'Rules for the Incommensurable'. *SubStance*, 112, 11–36.

McDonald, L., Moore, B. and Timoshkina, N. (2000) *Migrant Sex Workers from eastern Europe and the Former Soviet Union: The Canadian Case*, Ottawa, Status of Women Canada.

McKeganey, N. P. and Barnard, M. (1996) *Sex Work on the Streets: Prostitutes and Their Clients*, Buckingham, Open University Press.

Meaker, L. (2002) 'A Social Response to Transnational Prostitution in Queensland, Australia', in S. Thorbek and B. Pattanaik (Eds) *Transnational Prostitution. Changing Global Patterns*, London and New York, Zed Books.

Mezzadra, S (2010) 'Capitalism, Migration and Social Struggles: Towards a Theory of the Autonomy of Migration', in V. Squire (Ed.) *The Contested Politics of Mobility: Borderzones and Irregularity*, London, Routledge.

Mezzadra, S. and Neilson, B. (2008) Border as Method or the Multiplication of Labour. Transversal: Borders, Nations, Translations. European Institute for Progressive Cultural Politics, http: //eipcp.net/transversae/0608/mezzadraneil-son/en consulted on 3 March 2010

Miko, T. F. (2003) 'Trafficking in Women and Children: The US and International Response', in T. A. Troubnikoff (Ed.) *Trafficking in Women and Children: Current Issues and Developments*, New York, Nova Science Publishers.

Molina, F. P. and Janssen, M.-L. (1998) *I Never Thought This would Happen to Me: Prostitution and Traffic in Latin American Women in the Netherlands*, Amsterdam, Foundation Esperanza.

Monzini, P. (2005) *Sex Trafficking: Prostitution, Crime and Exploitation*, London, Zed Books.

Moore, H. L. (2007) *The Subject of Anthropology: Gender, Symbolism and Psychoanalysis*, Cambridge, Polity.

Morokvasic, M. (1984) 'Birds of Passage are also Women …'. *International Migration Review*, 18, 886–907.

Morokvasic, M. (2004) '"Settled in Mobility": Engendering Post-Wall Migration in Europe'. *Feminist Review*, 77, 7–25.

Murray, A. (1998) 'Debt-Bondage and Trafficking: Don't Believe the Hype', in K. Kempadoo and J. Doezema (Eds) *Global Sex Workers: Rights. Resistance, and Redefinition*, New York and London, Routledge.

Nagle, J. (2002) Book Review. *Signs: Journal of Women in Culture and Society*, 27, 1177–83.

Nash, J. C. (2006) *Practicing Ethnography in a Globalizing World: An Anthropological Odyssey*, Lanham, Plymouth; AltaMira Press.

Nencel, L. (2000) *Ethnography and Prostitution in Peru*, London and Sterling, Virgina, Pluto Press.

Nieuwenhuys, C. and Pécoud, A. (2007) 'Human Trafficking, Information Campaigns, and Strategies of Migration Control'. *American Behavioral Scientist*, 50, 1674–95.

O'Connell Davidson, J. (1998) *Prostitution, Power and Freedom*, London, Polity.

O'Connell Davidson, J. (2002) 'The Rights and Wrongs of Prostitution'. *Hypatia*, 17, 84–98.

O'Connell Davidson, J. (2006) 'Will the Real Sex Slave Please Stand Up?' *Feminist Review*, 83, 4–22.

O'Connell Davidson, J. (2010) 'New Slavery, Old Binaries: Human Trafficking and the Borders of "freedom"'. *Global Networks*, 10.

O'Neill, M. (2001) *Prostitution and Feminism. Towards a Politics of Feeling*, Cambridge, Polity.

O'Neill, M. and Berberet, R. (2000) 'Victimisation and the Social Organisation of Prostitution in England and Spain', in R. Weitzer, R. (Ed.) *Sex for Sale: Prostitution, Pornography and the Sex Industry*, New York and London, Routledge.

Ong, A. (2006) *Neoliberalism as Exception: Mutations in Citizenship and Sovereignty*, Durham and London, Duke University Press.

Orfano, I. (2003) 'Country Report Italy', in Payoke, T. O. ROAD and D. R. Draad (Eds) *Research Based on Case Studies of Victims of Trafficking in Human Beings in Three EU Member States, i.e. Belgium, Italy and The Netherlands*, Brussels, Commission of the European Communities, DG Justice & Home Affairs, Hippokrates JAI/2001/HIP/023.

Orsini-Jones, M. and Gatullo, F. (2000) 'Migrant Women in Italy: National Trends and Local Perspectives', in F. Anthias and G. Lazaridis (Eds) *Gender and Migration in Southern Europe*, Oxford, Berg.

Papadopoulos, D., Stephenson, N. and Tsianos, V. (2008) *Escape Routes: Control and Subversion in the 21st Century*, London and Ann Arbor, Pluto Press.

Papastergiadis, N. (2006) 'The Invasion Complex: The Abject Other and Spaces of Violence'. *Geografiska Annaler: Series B, Human Geography*, 88, 429–42.

Parrenas, R. S. (2001) *Servants of Globalization: Women, Migration and Domestic Work*, Stanford, Stanford University Press.

Pastore, F., Romani, P. and Sciortino, G. (1999) 'Italia nel sistema internazionale del traffico di persone. Risultanze investigative, ipotesi interpretative, strategie di risposta'. *Working Paper n.5*. Roma, Commissione per integrazione.

Pattanaik, B. (2002) 'Conclusions: Where Do We Go From Here?' in S. Thorbek and B. Pattanaik (Eds) *Transnational Prostitution: Changing Global Patterns*, London and New York, Zed Books.

Pearson, E. (2002) *Human Traffic, Human Rights: Redefining Victim Protection*, London, Anti-Slavery International.

Perera, S. (2002) What is a camp... ? *borderlands*, 1, http://www.borderlands.net.au/vol1no1_2002/perera_camp.html accessed 31 august 2010

Pettman, J. J. (1997) 'Body Politics: International Sex Tourism'. *Third World Quarterly*, 18, 93–108.

Pheterson, G. (1996) *The Prostitution Prism*, Amsterdam, Amsterdam University Press.

Phoenix, J. (1999) *Making Sense of Prostitution*, Basingstoke, Macmillan Press.

Phongpaichit, P. (1999) 'Trafficking in People in Thailand', in P. Williams (Ed.) *Illegal Immigration and Commercial Sex*, London and Portland, Frank Cass.

Pickup, F. (1998) 'More Word but no Action? Forced Migration and Trafficking in Women'. *Gender and Development*, 6, 44–51.

Precarias a la Deriva, C. (2004) *A la Deriva, por los circuitos de la precariedad feminina*, Madrid, Traficantes de Suenos.

Ratanaloan Mix, P. (2002) 'Four Cases From Hamburg', in S. Thorbek and B. Pattanaik (Eds) *Transnational Prostitution: Changing Global Patterns*, London and New York, Zed Books.

Raymond, J. (2002) 'The New UN Trafficking Protocol'. *Women's Studies International Forum*, 25, 491–502.

Regulska, J. (2001) 'Gendered Integration of Europe: New Boundaries of Exclusion', in H. M. Nickel and G. Jahnert (Eds) *Gender in Transition in Eastern and Central Europe*, Berlin, Trafo Verlag.

Ribeiro, M. and Sacramento, O. (2005) 'Violence against Prostitutes: Findings of Research in the Spanish-Portuguese Frontier Region'. *European Journal of Women's Studies*, 12, 61–81.

Rigo, E. (2005) 'Citizenship and Europe's Borders: Some Reflections on the Post-Colonial Condition of Europe in the Context of EU Enlargement'. *Citizenship Studies*, 9, 3–22.

Rigo, E. (2007) *Europa di confine: Trasformazioni della cittadinanza nell'Unione allargata*, Roma, Meltemi.

Rogaly, B. (2008) 'Migrant Workers in the ILO's "Global Alliance Against Forced Labour" Report: A Critical Appraisal'. *Third World Quarterly*, 29, 1431–47.

Roman, D. (2001) 'Gendering Eastern Europe: Pre-Feminism, Prejudice, and East-West Dialogues in Post-Communist Romania'. *Women's Studies International Forum*, 24, 53–66.

Rumford, C. (2006) 'Theorizing Borders'. *European Journal of Social Theory*, 9, 155–69.

Sacchetto, D. (2009) *Fabbriche Galleggianti. Solitudine a sfruttamento dei nuovi marinai*, Milano, Jacca Book.

Samarasinghe, V. (2008) *Female Sex Trafficking in Asia: The Resilience of Patriarchy in a Changing World*, New York, Routledge.

Sassen, S. (2000) 'Women's Burden: Counter-Geographies of Globalization and the Feminization of Survival'. *Journal of International Affairs*, 53, 503–24.

Sassen, S. (2006) *Territory, Authority, Rights: From Medieval to Global Assemblages*, Princeton, Princeton University Press.

Saunders, P. (2000) Migration, Sex Work, and Trafficking in Persons. http://www.walnet.org/csis/papers/saunders-migration.html, consulted 31 August 2010.

Scambler, G. and Scambler, A. (1997) *Rethinking Prostitution: Purchasing Sex in the 1990s*, London, Routledge.

Scarpa, S. (2008) *Trafficking in Human Beings: Modern Slavery*, Oxford, Oxford University Press.

Scully, E. (2001) 'Pre-Cold War in Traffic in Sexual Labour and Its Foes: Some Contemporary Lessons', in Kyle, D. and Koslowski, R. (Eds) *Global Human Smuggling: Comparative Perspectives*, Baltimore and London, The Johns Hopkins University Press.

Segrave, M. (2009) 'Order at the Border: The Repatriation of Victims of Trafficking'. *Women's Studies International Forum*, 32, 251–60.

Shannon, S. (1999) 'Prostitution and the Mafia: The Involvement of Organized Crime in the Global Sex Trade', in P. Williams (Ed.) *Illegal Immigration and Commercial Sex*, London and Portland, Frank Cass.

Sharma, N. (2003) 'Travel Agency: A Critique of Anti-Trafficking Campaigns'. *Refuge*, 21, 53–65.

Siemeienska, R. (2002) 'Economic Restructuring, Social Policies, and Women's Work in Poland', in R. Backer-Schmidt (Ed.) *Gender and Work in Transition: Globalization in Western, Middle and Eastern Europe*, Opladen, leske+budrich.

Skrobanek, S., Boonpakdi, N. and Janthakeero, C. (1997) *The Traffic in Women: Human Realities of the International Sex Trade*, London, Zed Books.

Smith, A., Pickles, J., Bucek, M., Begg, R. and Roukova, P. (2009) 'Reconfiguring "Post-Socialist" Regions: Cross-Border Networks and Regional Competition in the Slovak and Ukrainian Clothing Industry'. *Global Networks*, 8, 281–307.

Sossi, F. (2002) *Autobiografie negate: Immigrati nei lager del presente*, Roma, Manifestolibri.

Sutdhibhasil, N. (2002) 'Migrant Sex Workers in Canada', in S. Thorbek and B. Pattanaik (Eds) *Transnational Prostitution: Changing Global Patterns*, London and New York, Zed Books.

Thorbek, S. and Pattanaik, B. (Eds) (2002) *Transnational Prostitution: Changing Global Patterns*, London and New York, Zed Books.

Troung, T.-D. (1990) *Sex, Money and Morality: Prostitution and Tourism in Southeast Asia*, London, Zed Books.

UNICEF, UNHCHR and OSCE-ODIHR (2002) *Trafficking in Human Beings in South-eastern Europe*, Belgrade, UNICEF.

UNODC (2009) *Human Trafficking; Analysis on Europe*, Vienna, United Nations Office on Drugs and Crime.

USDOS (2006) *Trafficking in Persons Report*, Washington DC, US State Department

USDOS (2009) *Trafficking in Persons Report*, Washington DC, United States Department of State.

Van Der Veen, M. (2000) 'Beyond Slavery and Capitalism: Producing Class Difference in the Sex Industry', in J. Gibson-Graham, S. Resnick and R. Wolff (Eds) *Class and its Others*, Mineapolis and London, University of Minnesota Press.

Van Der Veen, M. (2001) 'Rethinking Commodification and Prostitution: An Effort at Peacemaking in the Battles over Prostitution'. *Rethinking Marxism*, 13, 30–51.

Walsum, S. K. V. and Spijkerboer, T. (2007) *Women and Immigration Law: New Variations on Classical Feminist Themes*, Abingdon, Routledge-Cavendish.

Walters, W. (2002) 'Mapping Schengenland: Denaturalizing the Border'. *Environment and Planning D: Society and Space*, 20, 561–80.

Weston, K. (2008) 'A Political Ecology of "Unnatural Offences": State Security, Queer Embodiment, and the Environmental Impacts of Prison Migration'. *GLQ: A journal of lesbian and gay studies*, 14, 217–37.

Wijers, M. and Lap-Chew, L. (1997) *Trafficking in Women, Forced Labour and Slavery-Like Practices in Marriage, Domestic Labour and Prostitution*, Utrecht, STV.

Wolkowitz, C. (2006) *Bodies at Work*, London, SAGE Publications.

Wright, M. (2006) 'Public Women, Profit, and Femicide in Northern Mexico'. *South Atlantic Quarterly*, 105, 681–98.

Zatz, N. D. (1997) 'Sex Work/Sex Act: Law, Labour, and Desire in Constructions of Prostitution'. *Signs: Journal of Women in Culture and Society*, 22, 277–308.

Index